MEMORIES OF OLD SMOKY

MEMORIES OF OLD SMOKY

EARLY EXPERIENCES IN THE GREAT SMOKY MOUNTAINS

CARLOS C. CAMPBELL

Edited by Rebecca Campbell Arrants

Preface by George W. Fry
SUPERINTENDENT (1963–69),
GREAT SMOKY MOUNTAINS NATIONAL PARK

OUTDOOR TENNESSEE SERIES
JIM CASADA, SERIES EDITOR

THE UNIVERSITY OF TENNESSEE PRESS
Knoxville

The Outdoor Tennessee Series covers a wide range of topics of interest to the general reader, including titles on the flora and fauna, the varied recreational activities, and the rich history of outdoor Tennessee. With a keen appreciation of the importance of protecting our state's natural resources and beauty, the University of Tennessee Press intends the series to emphasize environmental awareness and conservation.

Library of Congress Cataloging-in-Publication Data

Campbell, Carlos C. (Carlos Clinton), b. 1892.
Memories of Old Smoky: early experiences in the Great Smoky Mountains / Carlos C. Campbell; edited by Rebecca Campbell Arrants.—1st ed.
    p. cm.—(Outdoor Tennessee series)
  Includes bibliographical references (p. 209).

    ISBN 1-57233-373-1 (pbk.)

  1. Great Smoky Mountains (N.C. and Tenn.)—Description and travel.
  2. Great Smoky Mountains National Park (N.C. and Tenn.)—Description and travel.
  3. Campbell, Carlos C. (Carlos Clinton), b. 1892—Travel—Great Smoky Mountains (N.C. and Tenn.)
  4. Hiking—Great Smoky Mountains (N.C. and Tenn.)
  5. Camping—Great Smoky Mountains (N.C. and Tenn.)
  6. Great Smoky Mountains (N.C. and Tenn.)—Pictorial works.
  I. Arrants, Rebecca Campbell.
  II. Title.
  III. Series.

  F443.G7C325 2005
  917.68'89—dc22   2004018593

Contents

ILLUSTRATIONS

Map

Tables

SERIES EDITOR'S FOREWORD

Jim Casada

Carlos C. Campbell was a staunch son of the southern Appalachian up-country whose contributions as a writer and progenitor of the Great Smoky Mountains National Park merit not only remembrance but praise. He played a vital role in first promoting, then chronicling, the emergence of America's most popular national park, and his lifelong love affair with the Smokies conveyed an admirable sense of place and passionate attachment to one of the good earth's loveliest settings worthy of the most committed of conservationists.

Campbell's pioneering history *Birth of a National Park in the Great Smoky Mountains* (1960) gives an understanding of the sense of mission that motivated Campbell and a host of allies who worked tirelessly to make the park a reality. That comes in part from the author's firsthand experiences but also because the work conveys a closeness to the park and all it has always meant to those who cherish its wild reaches and remote fastnesses. While *Birth of a National Park* has, in some senses, been superseded by a pair of more recent treatments, Daniel S. Pierce's *The Great Smokies: From Natural Habitat to National Park* (2000) and Margaret Lynn Brown's *The Wild East: A Biography of the Great Smoky Mountains* (2000), it deserves careful consideration in any serious look at the history of the Great Smokies.

Also worthy of mention is the fact that the author, far from seeking literary fortune, made some laudable sacrifices to see *Birth of a National Park* become published reality. He took a leave of absence of several months from his career as an insurance agent in order to complete the work. While the volume did well, royalties from books published by university presses do not offer the sort of income to replace what he would have lost. The book was, in other words, a true labor of love.

Similarly, a second book from Campbell, his *Great Smoky Mountains Wildflowers: When and Where to Find Them,* is a delightful little spiral-bound handbook that reflects, in many senses, the man who was Carlos Campbell. (Coauthored with Aaron Sharp, Robert Hutson, and William Hutson, the book was originally published in 1962. It was updated and expanded in 1995, long after Campbell's death.) For many years it was among the University of Tennessee Press's most popular works. Indeed, folks connected with the press tell me it ranks, in terms of total sales, among their all-time bestsellers. Campbell clearly knew his subject intimately, had an encompassing passion for the Smokies and their flora and fauna, and in a quiet, unassuming fashion was anxious to share his passion with others. Characteristically, Campbell, as well as his co-authors, opted to forgo their royalties on *Wildflowers* in order to make the full-color work a bit more affordable to the public.

Everything Campbell wrote was done with care and is redolent of his beloved Smokies. He found numerous national outlets for his work and contributed articles to *The Playground* and *Journey's Beautiful,* popular travel magazines of the 1920s, on the Smokies and the movement to create a national park. In 1934, shortly after the park's establishment, he penned a piece for the *American Rifleman* entitled "The Great Smokies: A Big Game Preserve." What the average reader might not realize is that the source of its original appearance was and continues to be the house publication of the National Rifle Association. A year later his "Conquering the Crest of the Great Smokies" appeared in *American Forests.* The latter two pieces, in revised form, appear in the current work.

That brings us, after a brief trek down biographical byways, to this reprint of *Memories of Old Smoky.* In her editor's note introducing the book, Campbell's granddaughter Rebecca Campbell Arrants explains that he completed this book in 1967. According to her, publishers at that time rejected it outright, suggesting that "memoirs" did not sell well. Thankfully, literary tastes have changed, as is apparent by the recent success of somewhat similar books such as Johnny Molloy's *Trial by Trail* (1996), Harvey Broome's *Out Under the Sky of the Great Smokies: A Personal Journal* (2001), and Carson Brewer's *A Wonderment of Mountains* (2004).

In truth, speaking strictly on a personal basis, I have always found accounts of this sort fascinating. One of the most cherished items in my library of Appalachian literature, while it is by no stretch of the imagination a polished piece of writing, is Sam Hunnicutt's *Twenty Years Hunting and Fishing in the Great Smokies* (1926). Another book that draws me often to its pages is Felix Alley's *Random Thoughts and Musings of a Mountaineer* (1941). Throw in other books—such as Tom Alexander Jr.'s *Mountain Fever* (1995); Gary Carden's delectable *Mason Jars in the Flood & Other Stories* (2000), a work that one senses is almost entirely autobiographical in nature; and Harry Middleton's delightful *On the Spine of Time* (1991)—and it becomes increasingly obvious that, in yesteryear as well as today, books recounting experiences in the heart of the highlands have a special attraction. Certainly Campbell's *Birth of a National Park* holds a prideful place in this genre, and more than once over the years, as I perused its pages, a fleeting thought to the effect "this needs to be more widely available" has crossed my mind.

The present volume is in essence a collection of hiking, camping, and backpacking recollections. In that sense, it is a reflection of the man and his milieu. Campbell was among the founders of the Smoky Mountains Hiking Club, which continues going strong today; he logged upwards of five thousand miles on park trails; and he made an incredible eighty-five treks to his favorite destination, Mt. LeConte. The book opens with accounts of experiences along the trails and in remote campsites. To join Campbell vicariously on these long-ago trips by shank's mare (and in one instance, on horseback) is to tread literary trails of wonder. The short section on photography that follows reminds us that Campbell loved looking through a lens. He followed the light and recorded what he saw and experienced, not only in words but in visual form as well. Anyone who doubts Campbell's skills as a photographer need only note that he had eight photographs published in *National Geographic,* an accomplishment many would consider the pinnacle of achievement in the field.

In this regard, he reminds me of a contemporary of his (I suspect Campbell knew him reasonably well), who was a photographer and fellow promoter and lover of the Park. This was Bryson City, North Carolina's Kelly Bennett. How wonderful it would have been to accompany these men as they meandered through their beloved park, viewing and capturing it through the camera's lens over many decades. I remember as a boy looking at long, specially made wooden boxes holding "Doc" Kelly's images in the drug store he owned in Bryson City with awestruck wonder. And, like that of "Doc" Kelly, Campbell's way in chronicling the park visually deserves remembrance and praise.

But I wander astray, musing on matters in much the way Campbell loved to do as he sought solace in the remoteness of the Smokies. He joys in the "Solemnity of Silence," reminds us of the enchanting vagaries of weather in the mountains, and even shares some of the endearing characters of Appalachian fastnesses, such as the famed Walker sisters and bear hunter Uncle George Whaley, with us. We wander through high-elevation clouds with Campbell as our guide, share his enthusiasm for changeless yet ever-changing waterfalls, and savor a delightful little wildlife essay on "boomers" (the colloquial name for a now-endangered mountain squirrel).

In his preface to the original edition of this work, George Fry, who served as park superintendent for a number of years during the 1960s, refers to Campbell as one of the "hardy" individuals who led the fight for the creation of the Great Smoky Mountains National Park. Campbell was hardy in ways that far transcended the infighting and behind-the-scenes maneuvering that ultimately resulted in the creation of a national treasure in the southern mountains. A lean, lanky man whose stride ate up miles of rugged terrain in effortless fashion, Carlos Campbell belonged to the school of those who believed that, as Horace Kephart put it in such telling fashion, "in the school of the woods there is no graduation day." Campbell loved being in nature's classroom, continuing his lifelong studies at every opportunity, and in this book we are offered an engaging glimpse of "Old Smoky" as Campbell knew it. I've often said that there are those who are *of* the mountains and those who are simply *in* the mountains. Carlos Campbell epitomizes those belonging to the former breed, and as someone who shares his sense of connection to the high country, I'm delighted to welcome this work to a prideful place in the Outdoor Tennessee Series.

EDITOR'S NOTE

Rebecca Campbell Arrants

My grandfather Carlos C. Campbell wrote the original manuscript of *Memories of Old Smoky* in 1967. It was turned down for publication over thirty years ago with the explanation that though his other two books (*Birth of a National Park* and *Great Smoky Mountains Wildflowers*) had done very well, there was not a great demand for "memoirs." This was an immense disappointment to my grandfather, who sought to share some of his knowledge and experiences with those who might find them valuable and enjoyable.

A few copies of the manuscript were bound in its original typewritten format, with his handwritten notes of corrections and changes to be made still on the pages. These copies were given to family members and a few friends who have treasured them for years.

Memories of Old Smoky has within its covers the recounting of experiences and history. Some stories are of struggles and challenges; some are of indescribably beautiful vistas with fragile and ever-changing views. Some are poignant, some are humorous, but all are valuable and enjoyable to those with an interest in these wonderful mountains.

Minimal editing has been done with his manuscript. The corrections and changes noted by him were fixed, and the placement of a few of his stories have been rearranged into a more readable and organized format. Pictures have been added so that the reader may get a better idea of the times and in some cases see the subjects of his stories. Photographs that are not otherwise credited were made by Carlos C. Campbell.

Proceeds from the sales of *Memories of Old Smoky* are being shared with the Great Smoky Mountains Conservation Association so that Carlos C. Campbell's dedication to the promotion and preservation of the Great Smoky Mountains will continue.

September 2000

PREFACE

George W. Fry, Superintendent (1963–69)
Great Smoky Mountains National Park

This collection of personal experiences and observations of the Great Smoky Mountains was made over a period of about forty-five years and brought together in this fine book. Much of the information it contains was gathered before the Great Smoky Mountains National Park was established in June 1934 as the tenth largest in the national park system. The Great Smoky Mountains National Park lies astride the magnificent Appalachian Range near its southern extremity, between North Carolina and Tennessee. It is a region of great hardwood forests; high, rugged mountains; sparkling streams; deep valleys with wildflowers; and colorful shrubs in vast profusion and variety.

About half of the park is virtually untouched wilderness accessible by good roads and an excellent trail system culminating in the popular seventy-two-mile section of the Appalachian Trail that extends along the crest of the range from Davenport Gap to Fontana. It is located within a day's drive of half the nation's population, and more than six million visits were recorded in 1966, with again as many in 1967, surpassing attendance in any of the other national parks.

Sixty years ago this scenic mountain country was known to but a few hardy men and women who had settled and established small farms and lived off the land in near-complete isolation. Little had been written about this region except by a few land surveyors and scientists who had courage enough to penetrate the remote solitude of this heavily-forested wilderness to endure its hardships and to learn about its natural and cultural features.

Once these outstanding features were known to the outside world, the mountain barriers, which for years had isolated the settlers, began to break down. Electricity, the radio, and later the automobile all contributed to remove the isolation of these mountains and the people who had lived here for several generations, pursuing a hard but peaceful life.

It is fortunate for our nation that a group of far-seeing people of high ideals and great civic pride realized the importance of saving a part of this mountain wilderness for the people of America. They undertook the long, hard task of establishing in this area a national park. They contributed time, effort, and even personal funds to the planning of this park project, which we realize was a long and difficult one. Their efforts were rewarded by its completion. Its popularity eventually grew beyond all expectations, and it is the most-visited national park in our system.

Carlos C. Campbell, the author of this book, was one of those "hardy" individuals who was in the midst of the struggle to establish the Great Smoky Mountains National Park. He has hiked more than four thousand miles over the park's trail system with many of those miles logged before there were trails. On many of these trips he led famous conservationists and scientists who were later to join him in his enthusiasm and support for the natural significance of the Great Smoky Mountains.

He was on hand to help select and mark the route of the famous Appalachian Trail through the park, along with other members of the Smoky Mountains Hiking Club, adding to his intimate knowledge of the high country.

In 1965 he was presented the Horace Marden Albright Scenic Preservation Medal given through the American Scenic and Historic Preservation Society of New York for outstanding work in the field of conservation. His "Memories" contribute intimate experiences and additional information in natural resource conservation and reading enjoyment.

ACKNOWLEDGMENTS

Of the several deaths that have occurred in the Great Smokies during the past thirty-five years, most of them were caused by traffic accidents. There is, however, some special interest in the few nontraffic deaths.

Appreciation is hereby expressed to Mr. George W. Fry, superintendent of the Great Smoky Mountains National Park, for his letter of October 9, 1967, in which he supplied the exact names, dates, and some of the other details used in the foregoing brief descriptions of seven nontraffic deaths. My appreciation is also expressed to the following:

To Mr. John A. Harper, Jr., managing editor of the *American Rifleman,* for permission to use most of my article "The Great Smokies: A Big Game Preserve," which was published in the August 1934 issue of his magazine.

To Mr. James B. Craig, editor of *American Forests,* for permission to use most of my article "Conquering the Crest of the Great Smokies," which was published in the June 1935 issue of his magazine.

To Mr. Louis T. Iglehart, director of the University of Tennessee Press, for permission to use a few items about a subzero hike to Mt. LeConte that were used in my book *Birth of a National Park,* which was published in 1960 by the University of Tennessee Press.

Introduction

Lucky is the person who knew Old Smoky before, during, and after the establishment of the Great Smoky Mountains National Park. The "personality" of the area underwent numerous changes during the first twenty-five years after the park movement was launched in 1924. Most of these changes made it easier for the visitor to see and enjoy these rugged mountains, and to do so without damage to the natural beauty of the trees, shrubs, and wildflowers.

Looking backward on several hundred hiking, horseback, and motoring trips during a period of more than forty years brings memories tumbling one on the other. They are pleasant memories. Even though many of the experiences recalled herein involved periods of considerable discomfort (wet, cold, extreme thirst, much fatigue, and many sore muscles) they are all enjoyable in retrospect.

Only those trips in which there was some special interest have been used in this collection of stories. Several were selected because they contain some phase of nature lore. In others a touch of humor or some other human-interest sidelight prompted the selection.

A few of the recollections are recounted in the hope that they may serve to help other old-time hikers to recall these or other similar experiences of their own. It is hoped, too, that descriptions of some of the trips and the bits of outdoor philosophy may help young hikers—even those who have done little or no hiking in the Smokies—to get a general idea of what these picturesque and rugged mountains were like before the building of the graded trails along the eastern half of the park.

No attempt has been made to present the various items in chronological sequence. In most instances the time of occurrence has no significance. The presentation of "memories" has been divided into sections with some degree of similarity of subjects.

Every item herein presented is a true story. Most of them are based on my own personal experiences and observations, hence the first-person presentation.

Although many names of associates on various trips are given, no effort has been made to list all who were on certain trips. Many of the experiences, but by no means all of them, occurred on early trips of the Smoky

Mountains Hiking Club, which I helped to organize. It is not in any sense of the word intended as a history of hiking-club activities.

The names that are used are correct, but for obvious reasons, the identities of a few are not given. As has been stated in a popular television series, certain names have been concealed "to protect the innocent."

Thanks to the U.S. Board on Geographic Names, a branch of the Department of the Interior, who is the authority for the omission of the possessive apostrophe in such Great Smokies place-names as Andrews Bald, Abrams Falls, Cades Cove, Clingmans Dome, Porters Flats, Silers Bald, and others.

HIKING HIGHLIGHTS

Prepark Interest

Prior to the 1923–24 launching of the successful movement to establish a national park in the Great Smokies only a very small number of the people from Knoxville and nearby had any knowledge of, or interest in, these rugged mountains. A few employees and attorneys for owners of large tracts of land made exploring trips very early in the twentieth century. Most of the others who went into the mountains in those early days were trout fishermen and an occasional hiker-camper.

Even during the early years of the Great Smoky Mountains National Park many Knoxville residents didn't get very interested in exploring the Smokies. They were, in most cases, glad the park had been established, but that was about the extent of their personal interest.

Such was the attitude of Dr. Dan Welch, a teacher at Knoxville High School and minister of the Unitarian Church. About 1927 he moved to New England. Almost immediately he began to hear neighbors and other acquaintances brag about the grandeur of their mountains. The more of this he heard the more he regretted that he had not gotten personally familiar with the Great Smokies while he lived in Knoxville. He became enchanted because of his great distance from the Smokies.

On his next visit to Knoxville he asked me to take him on a hike to Mt. LeConte. Though it hadn't always been so, by this time that was all I needed. My wife had been telling friends that I was always ready for a trip to the Smokies "at the drop of a hat," that all I needed was an excuse, and if an excuse didn't occur to me soon enough, I would invent one.

So a hike to LeConte was arranged within a few days. My companions were Dr. Welch, his daughter Carolyn, my daughter Jean, my son Clinton, and a neighbor, June Woolrich. Although it was a beautiful June day when we started hiking, the picture changed quickly, and within a very short time we were hiking in a hard, brief summer rain. About the time we were getting dried out another shower descended upon us. However, we were approximately dry, again, by the time we reached LeConte Lodge. We wouldn't have wished for those showers, of course, but they were actually enjoyed by all of us, and the better views that we had from Cliff Top and Myrtle Point came as a bonus from the rains, since they cleared the air of the customary haze.

When Dr. Welch returned to New England, he felt that at long last he was able to do a little bit of bragging about the charm and grandeur of the Great Smokies. He could now hold his own with his northern friends the next time they started to rave about their mountains.

🍂   🍂   🍂

Much of the previously mentioned lack of interest was due to the great difficulty of even reaching the foot of the mountains. The few roads were of such poor quality that they hardly deserved the name "roads." Most of those who went beyond Pigeon Forge or Townsend either went by horseback or rode jolt wagons. Even when automobiles came into limited use, many of the roads were so narrow, crooked, and rough that it was almost impossible to get an automobile over them.

It was not unusual that when we had to lift an old car out of a rut, it was so deep that the axles were dragging. Another problem was that much of the road was so narrow that it was impossible for two cars to pass, with the result that one or the other would have to back up until it reached a spot that was wide enough for safe passage.

These necessary backups were usually made in good humor and without an argument. The story is told that on one occasion a mild conflict developed to the point where it appeared that it might not remain free from an actual argument, or possibly worse. Each motorist insisted that the other was the one who should do the backing, but with no successful resolution.

"If you don't. I'll have to do what my grandfather did," he threatened.

To prevent a conflict, motorist "B" then backed up a few hundred yards and pulled off to one side to permit the passing. As "A" pulled alongside, motorist "B" asked, "What was it that your grandfather did?"

"*He* backed up," replied motorist "A" as he sped away as fast as he could.

🍂   🍂   🍂

Shortly before 1912 some women from the national fraternity Pi Beta Phi rode horseback into Gatlinburg, where they hoped to enlist cooperation for their plan to establish a settlement school at which they would not merely teach the three R's but also revive the almost lost art of handicrafts. Much of the early interest in the Gatlinburg area was due to the work of the "Pi Phi" school.

Even with the many difficulties of approach, a few adventurous men did penetrate the wilderness areas that were completely unknown to most of their friends. Many of their trips lasted for several days, some with fishing as a major interest, and others going up to and then following the state line or main crest for several miles before going off to some North Carolina town from which the return to Knoxville could be made by train.

Among the friends who have told me of their Great Smokies exploits were Harry P. Ijams, S. A. Ogden, Gen. Frank Maloney, Charles I. Barber, Prof. S. H. Essary, and others, all of whom died some years ago. Other early explorers who were still living in 1967 include James H. Hickman, Claude M. Rawlings, Forrest Andrews, John A. Ayres, Paul M. Fink (of Jonesboro), and J. A. Fisher (of Maryville).

It is interesting to note that many of the early Great Smokies enthusiasts did not know, or remember, very much about specific points that they visited on their long hikes. Nor did they remember what streams or ridges they followed even in reaching peaks that they did know, such as Silers Bald.

The timber cutting and railroad building of the Little River Lumber Company served to stimulate some increase in hiking in the area from Sugarland Mountain westward to Thunderhead. It also led to the establishment of the summer colonies at and near Elkmont. It was through their trips to, and visits at, the Appalachian Club at Elkmont that Mr. and Mrs. W. P. Davis and Col. and Mrs. David C. Chapman first learned of the charm and grandeur of the Great Smokies. It was Mrs. Davis who suggested the desirability of having a national park in the Great Smokies, and Mr. Davis who launched the park movement. Colonel Chapman then led the movement to its successful conclusion.

My first trip, in the summer of 1922, into what is now the Great Smoky Mountains National Park was a two-week visit to Camp LeConte, a Boy Scout camp in the Wonderland Park section of Elkmont. At the time I was a scoutmaster. While there I participated in three hikes. The first was approximately along the bank of Laurel Branch, with not even a beaten path, much less a trail, to Laurel Falls. The first rattlesnake I ever saw was on this trip. My first close-up view of Mt. LeConte was from the crest of Sugarland Mountain, on my second Great Smokies hike. A dozen or more people made each of these hikes.

The third hike was very different. Bob Bruner and I arranged for an early breakfast so we could catch the logging train that left Elkmont shortly after daylight. It was pulled by a Shea engine, which had vertical driveshafts that permitted the engine to negotiate the sharp curves. As the train reached the steeper slopes it was necessary to use a number of switchbacks. Very soon, however, the terrain became so steep that even the Shea engines could not make it, and the flat cars that were to haul out their loads of logs had to be pulled farther up the mountain by a steel cable that was powered by a gasoline engine at the upper edge of the timber-cutting area. From that point Bob and I walked the remainder of the way to the main crest or state line, possibly less than a mile above the tracks of the cable car. We walked along the relatively level crest for a mile or so, then returned to meet an afternoon run of the cable car. We had no idea whatsoever just where we were, and I still do not know, except that it was somewhere between Clingmans Dome and Cold Springs Knob.

Although all three of these trips were mildly interesting, they did not create in my mind any very deep interest in the Great Smokies. There had been no breathtaking panoramas, with precipitous cliffs below us—nothing that could be classed as a "mountaintop experience." It was understandable, therefore, that I made no plans for further mountain hikes, and there was not another one for more than two years.

In the summer of 1924 Marshall A. Wilson, then boys' work secretary of the Knoxville YMCA, took a group of boys on a hike to Mt. LeConte. It proved to be so enjoyable that George F. Barber, physical director of the Y, began to plan a LeConte trip for men. His brother, Charles I. Barber, a

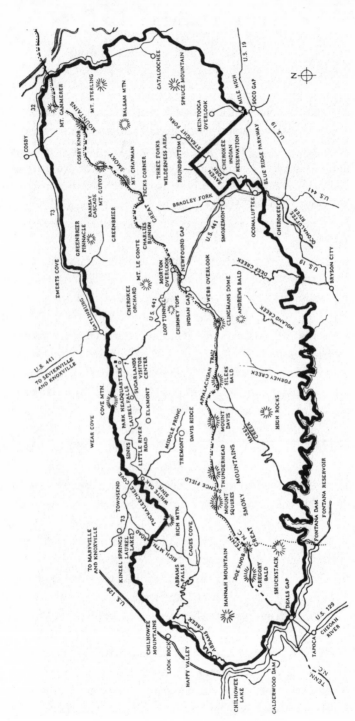

Great Smoky Mountains National Park

Hikers on the trail from the hiking club cabin to Fitified Spring and Brushy on November 6, 1938. In the background are Greenbrier Pinnacle, Mt. LeConte, and Mt. Chapman.

Glimpse of cloud-draped dining room at LeConte Lodge on Mt. LeConte, July 4, 1939.

prominent architect, invited me to make that hike with him. At the time I was assistant manager of the Knoxville Chamber of Commerce. I told him I was too busy—which was just my way of telling him that I was not interested. A few days later he renewed the invitation. Again, I was "too busy."

Mr. Barber realized that I was offering excuses, not reasons, and he changed his tactics. "You tell me that you are too busy to climb one of the grandest mountains of the east. If, instead, I had asked you to go with me to Yellowstone you would not be 'too busy' but you'd jump at the opportunity. Because this is something virtually in our backyard, you tell me you are too busy. Here you are at the Chamber of Commerce, supposedly in a position to tell people what we have around here, and you don't know a darned thing about it!"

I could not escape the realization that Mr. Barber was quite correct in his interpretation of my situation, and although I was a bit embarrassed, I agreed to climb Mt. LeConte with him and the other men who were going.

It was a glorious October day, which added greatly to the enjoyment of the trip. I can't remember very much, if anything, about the trip up the mountain, or even the trip down. But the thrilling views that we had from the two main vantage points were unforgettable. Cliff Top, where visitors could see the sunsets, is at the very brink of a cliff that drops off almost vertically for several hundred feet. This provided dramatic views of Chimney Tops, which was far below us, and Clingmans Dome and many ranges and ridges to the west and southwest.

From Myrtle Point, the sunrise peak of LeConte, we looked across the deep-cut gorges of Greenbrier to a veritable sea of mountains to the east and southeast. To the south we looked down on the sharp ridges of Huggins Hell and Alum Cave Bluff area, with several miles of the state line, or main crest, of the Smokies as a background.

Because of the spectacular quality of these views, Mt. LeConte (which stands off to the north of the main crest) has become recognized as "the grandstand of the Great Smokies."

At the time of the initial trip both observation points of Mt. LeConte were covered by thick growths of low shrubs. Cliff Top had a fine stand of dwarf rhododendron (*R. minus,* which was previously called Carolina rhododendron) with some myrtle mixed in. Myrtle Point derived its name from the very dense growth of mountain myrtle, or sand myrtle. We removed our shoes and "waded" in or on the carpet of myrtle, without ever touching the ground. Throngs of hikers in later years, however, wore down the beautiful shrubs on small areas of both observation points, with the result that we now walk on bare rocks for short distances.

While we were on Cliff Top, where we ate lunch and where an "official" picture of the group was made, it was agreed that this was such a wonderful experience that we must take steps to see that other such hikes would be made.

Those who made this initial trip to Mt. LeConte were Charles I. Barber, George F. Barber, Guy L. Barber, Carlos C. Campbell, A. L. Chavannes, Jim Eslinger (who helped carry Jim Thompson's heavy camera equipment), W. Baxter Gass, Miss Besse Geagley, Chas. Kane, Chas. Lester, W. H. McCroskey, T. S. McKinney, Neal B. Spahr, Douglas Smith, Miss Louise Smith, Jas. E. Thompson, Hugh M. White, Frank E. Wilson and Marshall A. Wilson.

This historic trip was made long before LeConte Lodge was built. The only shelter, a crude lean-to, was on the northern slope just below the summit of Cliff Top and approximately a half mile west of where LeConte Lodge later was built.

Almost immediately after the October 1924 trip to Mt. LeConte a series of meetings was held at the Chamber of Commerce with the result that the Smoky Mountains Hiking Club was organized. As would be natural, there were many suggestions for an appropriate name for the club. Mr. W. P. Davis, who had started the successful movement for a national park in the Great Smokies, advanced the suggestion that since most of the hiking would be done in the Smokies, the name should be the Smoky Mountains Hiking Club, and his suggestion was adopted.

A few hikes were made during the following weeks. Those made during 1925 were more or less on a hit-or-miss basis, most of them having been planned only a short time before the date for the trip. In the mean time, it was realized that the hikes should be planned longer in advance, and that leaders should be selected for each separate hike. Accordingly, a schedule was made for the entire spring, summer, and autumn of 1926, and a leaflet was prepared to give the dates, destinations, and leaders for the year's trips.

In retrospect, it seems strange that no winter trips were included in the 1926 program. For the mid-July hike from Cades Cove to Abrams Falls we were joined by about sixty members of Chicago's Prairie Club, under the leadership of O. M. Schantz. Mr. Schantz had been making occasional trips to the Great Smokies since 1912. While on the hike to Abrams Falls he expressed amazement that we had not been scheduling or conducting winter hikes. He told us that the Prairie Club's most enjoyable outings were those in winter months. So, more or less as an experiment, we arranged for two hikes per month throughout the year of 1927.

By that time we had learned that the printed schedule of hikes needed to present more information about each trip. Brockway Crouch, the president, asked me to write the descriptions. It was soon seen that the material was too much for a mere folder, with the result that the 1927 schedule was published in the first of the now-traditional handbooks.

The experiment in winter hiking proved to be quite successful. Members soon learned that, in most cases, it was actually easier to stay comfortable on a winter hike than on the same trip during the summer. Also, we learned that we could get many more fine panoramic views after the defoliation of the deciduous trees. Several years later I checked the attendance figures for the various seasons, and it came as quite a surprise to learn that there had been approximately twice as many hikers on winter trips as had gone on hikes for any other season.

Friends gave me a little razzing as I suggested that, when possible, over-night hikes—and even long one-day hikes—be scheduled for a date just a day or so before a full moon. That way we could have the benefit of moonlight for any night hiking that might be involved.

"What good would that do if it is cloudy or raining?" they chided.

Even so, the club did adopt the idea and soon found that it was very helpful, even when cloudy or raining. I recall that we were coming out of Greenbrier on a rainy night. To the surprise of some, there was still enough light coming through the clouds that we were able to follow a very dim (not graded) trail, even when it passed through an abandoned field in which weeds were knee-high.

My suggestion, however, was made primarily for the benefits we would get on clear nights. On one occasion I recall that some of the hikers who were first to get back down to Cades Cove were actually reading headlines from a newspaper when other hikers returned to the cars.

On another occasion we had selected a moonlight night for a hike to Gregory Bald. We started just after a rather late adjournment of a hiking club meeting, with the idea that we would get to watch a sunrise from the summit of Gregory the next morning. As usual, there was quite a bit of verbal horseplay as we made the long climb up Gregory Ridge trail. During this, I kept telling the others what a treat I was to have for breakfast, the treat being a can of prune juice. Much was said about that prune juice along the way—too much, perhaps, as I was to learn later.

We reached Moores Spring about an hour before sunrise. After getting drinks from that fine spring, we walked on, with the benefit of the nearly full moon, to the wooded crest just a few hundred yards east of the grassy summit. We left our packs there under the trees, where we had decided to have breakfast, and went on to the summit to await the sunrise. After watching a colorful sunrise we started back to our packs and our breakfasts. On the way, West Barber had quite a bit to say about my can of prune juice, but never enough to let me in on the secret that the others were sharing.

When I reached my own pack the first thing I noticed was the obviously empty juice can resting conspicuously on top of my pack. It was then that I realized that I had said too much about the treat that I had anticipated and I had to eat my breakfast without juice.

Plans for that initial hike for adults to Mt. LeConte included something of a warm-up trip for four members of the LeConte group—Jas. E. Thompson, Frank and Marshall Wilson, and Jim Eslinger. This little group started a day ahead of the others so they could make a picture-taking ascent of nearby Chimney Tops.

Photographic equipment and supplies of that period were very heavy, and the photographer, Jim Thompson, had to have the three other members of his group carry his load up the almost-vertical slopes of the twin-topped peak. They drove as far as possible up the Sugarland valley, only a mile or so above the present location of park headquarters. They then hiked on up the valley, with the base of Chimney Tops to their right and Mt. LeConte to their left, until they reached the old Grassy Patch Cabin—later designated as the Alum Cave Parking Area.

Leaving their bedding, extra clothing, and most of their food in the cabin, they hiked back down the valley to the foot of Chimney Tops, just above the present site of the Chimneys Campground, and started the very steep climb. At the time there was not even a beaten path up the side of the mountain, much less a graded trail. They had to push their way through the shrubs and other underbrush. Because of their heavy loads and the precipitous terrain their progress was so slow that it took *three hours* to climb a distance of less than two miles.

Marshall Wilson recalls that at one point he and his brother became separated. The tangle of rhododendron was so dense that Marshall actually was crawling along on *top of the shrubs!* Seeking to find his brother, he called to him to see if they could get back together. Much to his surprise, Frank was crawling along through the shrubs directly *under* Marshall.

While on the jagged Chimney Tops, Jim made pictures of the surrounding mountains, and made another in which he was looking down on the old "possession cabin" that Champion Fibre Company had built as a legal move to help establish a valid claim to the land. Then, when they got back down off the mountain, he made a now widely used picture of Chimney Tops in the background and the rustic cabin in the foreground.

The name Chimney Tops, or Chimneys—the names are used interchangeably—stems from the fact that there is a deep hole, approximately three or four feet in diameter, that starts from the west side of the higher peak and extends up approximately fifty feet to the top of the peak. It is likely that most people have supposed that the name relates to the general shape of the mountain. Based on shape, however, a more logical name would have been "Cathedral Spires." That is the title that I gave, in 1937 or 1938, to a picture of Chimney Tops as seen from Bear Pen Hollow. The shape of the mountain, plus the fact that a number of shapely hemlock trees were shown against the side of the peak, made Cathedral Spires all the more logical as the title for the picture. This picture was the Tennessee winner in a photographic contest conducted by the magazine *American Forests*.

After spending the night in the Grassy Patch Cabin—which was another of Champion Fibre's possession cabins and was sometimes known as Brackin's Cabin—the picture-making quartet hiked up the steep south slope of Mt. LeConte by way of Alum Cave Bluffs and joined the main group on Cliff Top. This was long before there was a graded trail in that area.

A few years later, after a beaten path had been made up the northeast slope of Chimney Tops, Frank Wilson set a very different record in climbing time for this mountain peak. Marshall stationed himself at a point at the base of the mountain from which he could see the summit, as Frank set out to see how quickly he could make the ascent. In a short twenty minutes he stood on the tip of the north peak and waved back to Marshall. This time he really was traveling light. His total wardrobe consisted of a pair of shorts, shoes, and socks, and he was carrying nothing. Even so, it is obvious that he ran much of the way.

While some hikers seek to see how fast they can go, others gain a greater pleasure from using a more leisurely pace. For the fast hikers it becomes largely a matter of physical endurance or an effort to be the "first one to the top." Members of the other group seek to see how much they can learn, and just enjoy spending more time in the high Smokies.

Several years ago I spent a considerable part of a certain hike with a high school boy who had just taken up hiking. A few weeks later he stopped me on a street corner and told me about another hike he had just made, adding proudly, "and I was the first one to the top!"

It was not my idea to be rude or harsh with him, but my immediate comment was "What a shame!"

He was, of course, surprised with my statement, and asked just what I meant. I reminded him that he had gone to the expense of the motor trip, but hadn't left sufficient time for really enjoying all of the interesting things that he might have seen.

"If it is just a physical stunt that interests you," I suggested, "why not go over and see how many times you can climb the stairway in the Hamilton Bank Building in an afternoon? There's nothing to see, and you can easily check your speed and endurance that way. But if you are going to the expense of a trip to the mountains, why not spend a little extra time and really enjoy it?"

It is understandable that youngsters are often inclined to stunting, but in most cases they soon get over that phase of it and do become good hikers.

Not all "speed" hikers are stunters, however. I recall that Hugh F. Hoss had long wanted to make the hike from Davenport Gap to Newfound Gap. At the time, in 1936, he was working as a deskman on the late shift at the *Knoxville Journal* when he began planning for that thirty-one miles in a continuous hike. His "training" for the trip was to run up and down the stairways of the Hamilton Bank Building, usually taking two steps at a time. On May 16 he left work just before midnight, and members of his family were to drive him to the starting point, Davenport Gap. He ate a midnight snack en route, and started the hike at 2:30 A.M. on May 17. He was carrying a very light pack, containing only a sweater, a poncho, a flashlight, a thermos of coffee, and a little food. He recalls that, with the aid of a flashlight, he saw an unusually early bloom of purple rhododendron along the way.

He ate breakfast at Low Gap, which point he reached a few minutes before his scheduled time. At Mt. Chapman he ate lunch and dozed for about thirty minutes, which put him a few minutes behind schedule. Although he did the climbing at a slow pace, he stepped it up a bit on the downgrades. This caused his feet to hurt, but he decided to push on despite the discomfort, and he was soon back on schedule.

He reached Charlies Bunion, four miles east of Newfound Gap, just as the sun was setting. He stopped there long enough to build a fire to heat water for coffee because his thermos had already been emptied. Refreshed by that stop, he made fast time the remainder of the way, and reached Newfound Gap at 8:15, just five minutes ahead of his scheduled time. It was, of course, already dark—and Hugh was depending upon catching a ride from the gap back to Knoxville—or, failing to find a ride, to spend the night in the gap.

Luckily, the first northbound car to come into the gap stopped when he waved to the driver. Luckily, also, the car was headed all the way to Knoxville. The driver, Joe Henry, accompanied by Mrs. Henry, readily gave Hugh the desired ride. It was several minutes later, however before they learned that both families lived in the Park City section of Knoxville, only about a block from each other.

Hugh is perhaps the first man to hike that thirty-one miles in a mere 17.75 hours.

At about the same time, or perhaps a few years earlier, Paul Hornburg, a young German who was then working at the University of Tennessee College of Agriculture, undertook to hike the western half of the Smokies, a distance of forty-one miles, in a single continuous trip. The only thing that I can recall is that Paul did complete the trip, but not quite as he had planned it. He was so near complete exhaustion that he actually crawled the last few miles—a clear case of dogged determination!

Another trip—entirely different in many respects—is recalled. This was a three-day horseback trip along the eastern half of the Smokies. When I was making arrangements for the horses, their owner expressed surprise that we wanted them for three days. "You can make it easily in two days," he said.

"Yes, I've hiked it in two days, with snow on the ground," I replied, "but that is not the point. We want to spend three days in the high Smokies."

Members of the party were Dr. William F. Hutson, his sister, Miss Mary Hutson, Jas. E. Thompson, Bill Tracy, and me. It was the first time Miss Hutson had ever ridden horseback on a mountain trail, and she was afraid that she couldn't last through such an ambitious trip. But when we explained that we never rode faster than a walk, and that we frequently got off and walked for a few minutes, she accepted our invitation, still a bit skeptically. She got along so nicely that she gladly joined us on several later horseback trips.

Still another case where a leisurely trip was planned and carried out: Mr. and Mrs. A. B. Crandall, of Akron, Ohio, spent ten full days along the main crest from Deals Gap to Davenport Gap, some seventy-two miles. They knew that they could have done it in five days, but they wanted the enjoyment of spending ten days in such interesting country. More about their trip is given later.

As already implied, I am by choice a very slow hiker. This is indicated by the fact that in climbing Mt. LeConte my normal time for the ascent is four or five hours. Only once did I ever make the climb in less than three hours, and I have spent as much as seven hours on the trail, but that was with a group of botanical friends who were doing a lot of botanizing along the way.

DR. PALMER'S TRIP

One of the speakers for the 1927 meeting of the East Tennessee Education Association was Dr. E. Laurence Palmer, a member of the faculty at Cornell University and associate editor of *Nature Magazine*. While in Knoxville he was also the speaker for the civic club of which I was a member. I recall that he had used a live snake in that talk, and that I carried the snake as Dr. Palmer and I walked down the street after the club meeting—and that the snake crawled up between my shirt and coat and then down my coat sleeve—which fact is purely incidental.

As is recounted in *Birth of a National Park,* an effort was made to get every important visitor—especially those who might help to give some publicity to the park movement—to make a trip into the Great Smokies. So as Dr. Palmer and I walked down the street I invited him to accompany me on a trip to Mt. LeConte.

"There's nothing I'd like better," Dr. Palmer replied, "but I have an appointment to spend tomorrow with Dr. L. R. Hesler." Dr. Hesler, a Cornell graduate and personal friend of Dr. Palmer, was then head of the Department of Botany at the University of Tennessee.

"Well, we'll just take Dr. Hesler with us to LeConte," I replied.

As proof that Dr. Palmer did actually want to make the LeConte trip, he readily agreed that he would go with me if Dr. Hesler would join us. Not merely did Dr. Hesler join us, but so did Brockway Crouch, another hiking friend. So the next morning the four of us had an early—about 4:30 A.M.—breakfast at an all-night lunch counter and hurried on our merry way toward the mountains.

It was a warm and clear day, on the thirty-first of October. We ate our sandwich lunches as we sat, in our shirtsleeves, on Cliff Top of Mt. LeConte. The views from this sunset point were superb, doubly so because much of the colorful autumn foliage was still in evidence. We then hiked eastward along the crest of the mountain almost a mile to Myrtle Point, the sunrise peak. If possible, the views there were even more enjoyable. They were the same panoramic views that thrilled the little group of pioneer hikers on that first LeConte hike almost exactly three years earlier. Efforts to describe them fall far short of what one experiences at such spectacular spots.

Then, as though I had just thought of the idea, I suggested that the readers of *Nature Magazine* would enjoy reading his account of that trip. Dr. Palmer probably never knew that it was this idea that caused me to extend the invitation in the first place. After a moment's thought, he agreed that it might be worthwhile.

"If you will write the story, the Chamber of Commerce [of which I was manager] will furnish the pictures," I said by way of promoting the idea. Not merely did he agree to write it, but he sent the manuscript for my review, explaining that with so little information he would be likely to include some statement that might not be correct. It was an excellent story, and needed only minor corrections, which he readily made.

The next I heard was that he was going very soon on his sabbatical leave, and that I should send the pictures, when called for, to Dr. Richard Westwood, editor of *Nature Magazine.* After several weeks Dr. Westwood wrote, asking that I send six pictures. As was my practice in such situations, I sent twelve carefully selected views, making certain that some were horizontal in shape and others vertical. This practice was followed because I felt sure that any editor is likely to eliminate at least one or two pictures, just to show that he is making the selections. In my Chamber of Commerce work I made wide use of pictures, usually spending from two hundred to three hundred dollars per year for that effective way of publicizing the Great Smokies and our effort to get our national park established.

Dr. Palmer's interesting story was scheduled for publication in the June 1928 issue of *Nature Magazine.* Although Dr. Westwood had asked for only six pictures—and I had sent twelve—he used nine with the story!

Under normal circumstances this would be the logical place to end this little story. Unfortunately, the circumstances here were something less than normal. I had tendered my resignation from the Chamber of Commerce post about the time that the pictures were paid for and mailed to Dr. Westwood. It became effective on March 1, 1928—exactly eight years after starting as assistant manager of the organization. Just try to imagine my surprise when about a month later I received a letter from Dr. Westwood telling that my Chamber of Commerce successor had written to *Nature Magazine* asking for the immediate return of the twelve Great Smokies pictures that I had sent to him. This, mind you, was actually before the scheduled time for their publication.

Dr. Westwood was, quite naturally, somewhat bewildered. He said that when he agreed to publish Dr. Palmer's story, he had expected that it would be appreciated by the people of the Knoxville area, as well as by general readers of the magazine. But that with such a letter from the Chamber of Commerce it left plenty of room for doubt about any possible local appreciation. In my reply I told Dr. Westwood that the pictures had been bought specifically for his use and that they had already been paid for. I further told him that I could give him the names and addresses of forty or fifty widely known easterners who were familiar with the intense interest in the Great Smokies by Knoxville people, and that the publication of the article would, indeed, be greatly appreciated. This seemed to convince him that the newly appointed Chamber of Commerce manager had not correctly represented the people he was supposed to be serving. It is of some interest that after he had been manager of the chamber for a year he actually boasted that during that year he had spent only six dollars for pictures. It is possible that someone had told him that I had been too "extravagant" in the use of pictures.

This, then, is really the end of the story about Dr. Palmer's enthusiastic report on his trip to Mt. LeConte.

THE WILDERNESS HIKE

In August of 1932 a party of nine members of the Smoky Mountains Hiking Club made what is still believed to be the first continuous hike from one end of the Great Smokies to the other. It became my privilege to write a detailed account of our trip. A condensed version of the story was published in the June 1935 edition of *American Forests*, under the title "Conquering the Crest of the Great Smokies."

The following account of that trip is based on the published story, but with a few omissions, still fewer additions, and a small amount of other editing that was needed because of the passage of time.

Up to 1932 very few hikers seriously considered traversing the entire main crest of the Great Smoky Mountains National Park in a single trip. The odds against success were too great—odds which mounted with each successive failure. Anyone who had sampled even for a day or two the untrailed way along most of the high crest, had challenged its ruggedness, had battled its junglelike undergrowth—all the while faced with the serious, sometimes desperate, problems of maintaining a water supply—knew the extent of these odds. Consequently, the inclination was to look upon such a venture as foolhardy at best.

We knew this. We knew also that grim failure had overtaken the only two parties within our knowledge to attempt the conquest. We had seen exhaustion written deeply in the faces of those who had tried it; we had looked with some strange emotion upon their clothing, torn to shreds by the unyielding undergrowth of rhododendron and mountain laurel; we had listened to their tales of chilling mid-summer rain, and about sleet that lay two inches deep on the ground. But for some reason we were not dismayed. The challenge of those failures could not be ignored, but it made us more determined than ever to conquer the crest of the Smokies.

There were nine of us, all members of the Smoky Mountains Hiking Club. In alphabetical order they were Walter M. Berry, Harvey B. Broome, Herrick B. Brown, Carlos C. Campbell, Charles Cornforth, E. Guy Frizzell, Charles Gibson, Warner Hall, and Carter Whittaker. We gave ourselves eight days in which to cover the thirty-one miles to Newfound Gap, 5,045 feet above sea level, and our announced destination. Among ourselves, however, we cherished the secret hope that we would get through to Deals

Gap, seventy-two miles from our starting point—seventy-two miles in eight days, an average of nine miles per day. That is a moderate distance for experienced hikers, but as any mountain hiker knows, a mere statement of mileage means little when such a dim-trailed way is concerned. The character of the terrain is vastly more significant in many cases; so is the presence of water, or the lack of it. Weather plays a hand, and so does luck.

Needless to say, our plans were carefully made. Particularly did we give serious attention to our packs, for the weight of these could spell the difference between success and failure. After much effort we managed to hold them to about sixty pounds each. Food and general equipment were apportioned equally as to weight and bulk, and so arranged that no one man would carry all of the bacon, another all of the dehydrated foods and so on around. As a substitute for water we included a quantity of canned goods because those who have fought their way along the crest of the Smokies know the difficulty of descending its slopes to find a supply of water.

So, when we set out one Sunday morning in August, it was with the feeling that we were organized to succeed. Our fate then rested in the hands of the elements and upon our own pack-burdened shoulders.

Our send-off was a memorable one. Other members of the club accompanied us as far as White Rock (later Mt. Cammerer), the first peak on our route. This they did as a tribute to our ambitions. Unfortunately this honor nearly ruined us. Our escorts, without packs, set a fast pace that we attempted to follow, and, as a result, after an hour of hiking and with White Rock still 2,500 feet above us, we began to lag behind. Finally, we found ourselves disposing of certain personal belongings to lighten our load. I am frank to admit that at one time I was so completely whipped that I would have turned back except for the fact that those ahead of me were depending upon food that was in my pack. There were others, too, who felt much the same way about it.

We made it, though, after a long session with the scorching afternoon sun. But we didn't feel much like conquerors. The torture of that climb had subdued our enthusiasm. Yet, as we watched the evening shadows lengthen from our 5,025-foot perch, and as we looked at that 360-degree panorama, we felt well repaid for the day's ordeal. Give up the trip? Never! We were conquerors again! The Smokies had challenged, and we, nine strong, had accepted! *Forward!*

From White Rock our route was to follow the Appalachian Trail, a continuous footway along the crest of the mountains from Maine to Georgia. The seventy-two miles of jagged state-line crest through the Great Smokies is the roughest and highest portion of this two-thousand-mile trail, and was one of the few sections where much of the way was still in a wilderness condition.

We had expected to reach Low Gap, three miles to the west, for our first camp, but darkness prevailed, and we spent that first night a mile short of the day's goal. However, we had breakfast at the gap on Monday morning. We filled our canteens and the canvas water bag, and started westward on a fairly good trail. But the trail did not serve us very far, and we soon were fighting our way laboriously through a maze of rhododendron and laurel, with a few saw briers interspersed for good measure. Sometimes we were on the state-line ridge crest; at other times we found better going on the Tennessee side. But it was slow travel no matter where we went, and very rough. Our packs were continually hanging on the underbrush, as was our clothing.

We pushed on until darkness was only an hour away, hoping against hope for a suitable campsite. Apparently none existed, so we staked our tents in the wilderness, away from any water, away from comfort, and away from everything but rhododendron. To conserve our scant supply of water, we warmed canned foods before a small fire so we would not have to use extra water for cooking. Then we turned in, but not until we had discussed plans for the next day. They were vague, for the country ahead was completely unknown to any of us. But one thing was certain: we had to find water. Already this problem was causing us great concern.

There was nothing to cause us to linger the next morning, so we made an early start. Soon we were out of the maze of underbrush and out into an open area caused by the lumberman's ax, and the fire that had followed. We paused for a moment to get our bearings, now that we could see something other than rhododendron, and found the view to be intriguing. Mt. Sterling was to the south, across the gorge of Big Creek, and was an impressive sight. Better still was the creek itself, for we could see its water. To the west loomed Mt. Guyot, the objective we had hoped to reach the night before.

Blackberries and huckleberries were plentiful, and so were the bear "signs." We did not see a bear, but we knew they had been around. Bears do like berries!

The sun shone down upon us with a vengeance. Not a cloud was in the sky. Nor were there any trees to shade us occasionally—only the charred remains of trees over which we were forced to climb, or go around. This was on the North Carolina side, so we tried to use the virgin forests on the Tennessee side but soon found the slope too steep for good hiking, and the undergrowth too thick. We then returned to the blistering sun of the open spaces where we plodded wearily along.

⌒   ⌒   ⌒

By careful use of water during the previous day and night we still had a pint or so between us. We considered descending to Big Creek, in plain sight below us, but we knew that it would involve a hard half-day's trip. I rather suspect, too, that had we succeeded in reaching it, many strong arguments would have been advanced for abandoning our planned conquest. Once off that sun-baked ridge, with our enthusiasm at low ebb, it would have been extremely difficult to return through the jungle that covered the side of the mountain. So we decided to push on, staking our chances on reaching the spring near Mt. Guyot.

It was time for lunch, but what we wanted most was water, not food. We knew that we could not expect to find water on the burned-over side, so we swung over to the steeper, tree-clad Tennessee slope. There was a chance we might find water there, although a very slim chance. At first the prospects were discouraging—the soil was bone dry. A little later we found slight traces of moisture under the leaves. Hope sprang up again.

Every canteen was now empty, as was the canvas bag and the situation became desperate. "I'm going down for water!" was the sudden announce-ment of Herrick Brown, the youngest member of the group. I wanted water just as badly as he did, but I was well nigh exhausted and needed rest even before water. So we let him go, after giving him all the canteens and the water bag. We even made up a pot of all of our loose change—and later calculated that he could have bought a similar quantity of a famous Cosby product with the money we gave him.

There was nothing for the rest of us to do but wait—and hope. Cans of kraut and grapefruit were opened; our throats were too parched for anything else. The slight relief this gave us more than justified the added weight of the canned goods.

We continually called to the water-searcher, but no sound came back. Minutes seemed hours, and finally our throats became so dry we could no longer call. Then we heard it, an indistinct call from below. We answered, as loudly as dry throats would permit, seeking to guide our companion back to where we waited so hopefully. Then, sooner than we expected, he came into view, with a big smile on his face and the moisture-covered water bag slung over his shoulder.

With our thirst once again quenched, we proceeded along the remainder of that desolate waste. Its name, Hell Ridge, described it adequately and accurately. In fact, that is when the ridge got its name! Even the cutover sections that the forest fire had missed were barren. At an elevation of 5,900 feet, just before we again reached a virgin forest, we found and killed a big rattlesnake. We were told later by Park Naturalist Arthur Stupka that this was a new high elevation for a rattler in the Smokies.

As we entered the beautiful forest at the shoulder of Old Black, we felt a new appreciation for the heroic work done by leaders of the park movement. It could not immediately restore beauty to Hell Ridge, but it could, and did, prevent other parts of the Smokies from meeting similar fates.

Because of the extremely slow pace on this third day of our trip, it was somewhat after dark before we reached the Guyot spring. Even after a good night's sleep we were still in need of rest, and being further tempted by the sheer beauty of the spot, we lingered quite a while at the camp on Wednesday morning. Such luxury was a treat for our weary bodies. Then we climbed the steep slope up to the summit of Mt. Guyot, where the elevation is 6,621 feet. This, the second highest peak of the Smokies, was named for Arnold Guyot, who made careful and remarkably accurate elevation measurements of scores of peaks and gaps in the Great Smokies before Civil War days. From this vantage point, we saw much of the entire park. After drinking in the views for an hour or so the clouds descended and obscured most of the surrounding peaks, so we resumed our journey—this time in a leisurely fashion. We were again in familiar territory! And we knew we had plenty of time in which to reach our next camp before dark.

Our route was over what ordinarily would be termed a very poor trail; some would hesitate to call it a trail at all. But in comparison with what we had just been through, it seemed like a highway. True, we had to crawl through or around an occasional windfall, and branches from the side switched us at almost every step, but there was a recognizable path much of the way.

We reached the 6,430-foot summit of Mt. Chapman in time for lunch and were rewarded by some of the finest views to be had on the entire state-line crest. This mountain is named for Col. David C. Chapman, whose ten years of leadership and tireless effort had brought the establishment of the park.

Suddenly it began to rain, and we stretched our ponchos to keep us dry and warm during the remainder of our lunch. How welcome that rain would have been twenty-four hours earlier! It stopped as we reached Mt. Sequoyah, named for the inventor, or developer, of the Cherokee Indian alphabet, but the wet branches that we encountered kept us drenched just as thoroughly.

Before leaving Mt. Sequoyah we checked carefully to be sure that we turned off at the correct place. We knew that what appeared to be the main range at the western end of Mt. Sequoyah was only a side ridge dropping off into Tennessee—and because it causes so much confusion to hikers is known as Old Troublesome. The state line, and water divide, turns down the south slope of Sequoyah and is not easily recognizable until just before reaching Copper Gap. It is one of the most confusing points on the state line, but we were on a sharp lookout for it. As we climbed along the rim of the steep ledges up from Copper Gap to Eagle Rocks the clouds began to lift, and we could again see some of the grandeur of the surrounding mountains.

Immediately following a rain is the very best time to see the Great Smokies. The characteristic haze, from which the range gets its name, is washed away, leaving the landscapes much clearer. On Eagle Rocks we were treated to spectacular sights such as only devotees of wilderness trails are privileged to see. Neighboring peaks, peeping above solid banks of white clouds, stood out in bold relief. A riot of color, beggaring any effort to describe, adorned the western sky.

We had planned to go on to the junction of the state line and Hughes Ridge, but the surroundings at Eagle Rocks were so very pleasing that we could not leave. After finding water within two hundred yards of the crest, we decided to camp there. It was difficult to go about such prosaic tasks as pitching tents and hunting for dead wood when each one of us much preferred to stand on the brink of that overhanging cliff and drink in the glory of that sunset. The situation was made even worse when Carter Whittaker did just that! To see that red ball of fire sinking behind mighty Mt. LeConte was well worth all that it had cost us in physical agony to reach Eagle Rocks —and especially just when we did.

When we finally did get underway on Thursday morning, we did not fill our canteens because it was well known to hikers that one of the most dependable springs in the high Smokies—at the junction of Hughes Ridge and the state line—was just a mile or so ahead of us. We still had enough to carry without packing water unnecessarily. But when we reached that spot, just before noon, we found that the "dependable" spring was dry! We had to go a mile farther down into North Carolina before we found water. After that experience we took nothing for granted and always carried a good supply of water.

Leaving Hughes Ridge and following the Appalachian Trail markers at a most confusing turn, we entered upon the most jagged, irregular crest of the main ridge of the Great Smokies. Quite appropriately, a ten-mile section of it is called the "Sawtooth Range." We descended along the knifelike crest for a few hundred feet of elevation only to climb back just as high or higher to get over the next "tooth" in that long "saw." At one place our descent was so steep that we pitched our packs down ahead of us to prevent them from bumping on the cliff back of us and throwing us off balance.

Throughout the next five miles we learned how elusive a mountain peak can be. We were headed toward Laurel Top, highest of the numerous "teeth" in the range. After crossing six or eight knobs, we began to feel that the next one, which we could see occasionally through the foliage, would be Laurel Top, only to find another high one between Laurel Top and us. When we finally did reach Laurel Top, the panorama that spread out before us was a suitable reward for the tedious approach. We counted fifteen separate ranges in that sea of mountains. Much of the Cherokee Indian Reservation, which borders the park on the south, was also seen.

Our fifth camp, on Thursday night, was at False Gap, about a mile west from Laurel Top. We can never forget that camp because of the "visitors" we had there. No, they were not other hikers; I wish they had been. It was our worst encounter of the trip with "punkies," or "no-see-ums," or tiny black gnats. By whatever name you call them, their bite is just as irritating. The sleep we got that night must be credited to the special insect-repelling salve that we had brought along, or to near exhaustion—or both. We were thankful that there are no mosquitoes in the higher elevations of the Smokies!

By this time we were beginning to wish for the waterfalls and graceful cascades that punctuate the six hundred miles of turbulent streams a bit lower on the mountainsides. Five days in the mountains without seeing a single pool in which a rainbow or speckled trout might be seen! There were flowers along our route, to be sure, some growing from tiny crevices of the sheer cliffs. It was not, however, a one-sided exchange. While we had missed the beauty of the crystal-clear streams, we had enjoyed the many sweeping panoramic views.

We hurried through our breakfast and were on our way early Friday morning for the first long day's hike of the trip. We covered more than ten miles that day, over the remainder of the Sawtooth Range, a delightful bit of rugged wilderness. The crest was steep and jagged, with sides dropping off abruptly below us. Without its forest cover it would have been too severe to be beautiful; but it was truly beautiful with the blanket of trees and shrubs growing from the carpets of deep mosses and ferns. With low-hanging clouds sweeping about us, protecting us from the heat of the sun, we made good time. Then, to our amazement, a high ridge to our right and above us became visible through a rift in the clouds. What could it be? We knew full well that there should be no high ridge on either side of us at this point.

Suddenly it dawned upon us that we had gotten off the state line and were down on a side ridge in North Carolina. Had such a thing happened on that torturous Tuesday along Hell Ridge I'm afraid there would have been no retracing of steps. But here we laughed it off and turned back up the ridge.

Just before noon, as we neared the end of the much-notched Sawtooth Range, we came into another, but much smaller, fire-devastated area. This fire also had followed closely upon the heels of the timber cutters. There are few such sections in the Great Smokies, and only two along the state line. The highest point in this fire scald bears the quaint appellation "Charlies Bunion." The thrilling views it offers help to make one almost forget the ugliness that was left by the fire.

We picked Charlies Bunion for our lunch site. With clouds hanging overhead to protect us from what otherwise would have been a scorching sun, the prospects for a pleasant rest were good. At least, that's what we thought. But before we had finished digging into our packs for the food, there were significant rumblings coming from the direction of Mt. LeConte, the towering and majestic peak on the Tennessee side. Quickly the storm broke upon us in all its fury.

This was no ordinary rain. It was swept horizontally, and sometimes upward, by a stiff gale. Our only recourse was to get moving. There was no keeping dry. With the upward sweep of the rain our ponchos became just so much excess baggage.

Lightning flashed alarmingly close as we stumbled through the maze of fallen tree trunks that had been left by the fire. Despite the fact that we were chilled to numbness by the rain, this was a thrilling experience. The storm subsided as we reached the next virgin forest. In a short time we climbed the steep grade that leads up to Jump-Off, a spur of Mt. Kephart. This is described by many as providing the most spectacular views in the Great Smokies. Then we turned our faces toward Newfound Gap, only three and a half miles away, which was our *announced* destination.

There, at an elevation of 5,045 feet, was a highway connecting with Gatlinburg, the park headquarters village just seventeen miles from us.

At Clingmans Dome (6,643-foot elevation) on August 13, 1932. This is the highest point on the two thousand miles of the Appalachian Trail (from Maine to Georgia) as well as the highest point in the Great Smokies. Front row, from left to right: Carter Whittaker, Harvey Broome, Warner Hall, Walter Berry. Back row, from left to right: Charles Cornforth, Charles Gibson, Carlos Campbell, Herrick Brown, Guy Frizzell. (Photo by Walter Berry)

Under construction at this time was also a highway to the Cherokee Indian Reservation, the same distance down on the North Carolina side.

Having reached our original destination ahead of time, we were by that time determined to go on in an effort to realize our secret hope of a seventy-two-mile continuous hike. But the temptation of soft beds and fancy food, available at Gatlinburg, was great. Faltering members argued that we could return the next morning after a good night's rest and continue the remainder of the trip. Of course we could, but would we? We dared not again become contaminated by civilization—not if the seventy-two miles of the crest line of the Smokies were to be covered in one continuous trip. Thus, with much reluctance, we again headed westward for another, but easier, forty miles of hiking.

The climb up across the shoulder of Mt. Mingus was steep and difficult, but we made it. We also made it on to what we called "Little Indian Gap," where we camped Friday night. On Saturday morning we made the steep ascent to Clingmans Dome, the highest point on the entire Appalachian Trail as well as the highest in the Smokies. The elevation there is 6,643 feet. We ate lunch there as we waited hopefully for the clouds to disperse so we could enjoy the views from the old wooden tower that rose just above the tops of the dense stand of balsam (Fraser fir) trees. But luck was not with us. The clouds remained, and we did not get to enjoy any of those sweeping panoramas. But we did get a picture of the bewhiskered group standing by an elevation marker.

Being easier of access and travel, this part of the Smokies is more frequently visited than is the rougher section we had just traversed. During the first six days the only people we had seen were the few motorists in Newfound Gap. But on Saturday we met two groups of men on the trail: a party of five hikers from Bryson City and two Park Service employees who were clearing trails. About two miles west of the dome we noted the last of the red spruce trees. Here, in the heart of the Southland, is the southernmost habitat of this tree that is also native to New England and Canada.

On Silers Bald, whose high, grass-covered summit usually rewards the hiker with superb views, we had only a fleeting glimpse through the shifting, low-hanging clouds. So we continued on to Buckeye Gap, where we spent the seventh night, after having made twelve miles of hiking for the day.

On Thunderhead, another treeless "bald," elevation 5,530 feet and covered mostly by grass, we enjoyed a few glimpses of charming Cades Cove, a long, level valley surrounded by a wall of mountains. By the time we reached the western end of this mountaintop meadow, the clouds had cleared, and we enjoyed a good rest, stretching ourselves out upon the carpet of turf. We wondered about the age-old mystery concerning the cause of these "balds."

✿   ✿   ✿

Even after we had decided to extend our hike to cover the entire length of the park, we still had hoped to complete it within the originally planned eight days. But by now it was beginning to be obvious that an extra day would be needed. This presented a serious problem for us. This time it was a food shortage, but it was about to become as serious as was the water shortage of our third day. We had already been rationing our diminishing supply. By Sunday we were even dividing such small items as crackers, but we continued hiking in the hope that we might be able to get a little food at the lone herder's cabin that remained at the edge of Russell Field, only a short distance from our trail.

As we approached Fondes Cable, the herder, we asked if he had any eggs or chickens that he would sell us. "Hell, no! I ain't got nothin' but sow-belly, 'taters, and meal," he answered. We were, indeed, glad to get about a gallon of potatoes, a gallon of coarse meal, and about a pound of fat bacon—so fat that there was not a single streak of lean in it. Believe it or not, that extremely simple food tasted like a banquet to us after having been on half rations for more than a day. We were becoming a part of this "land of do-without." (The early settlers of these remote mountain coves had to grow or make almost everything they used or do without them. There were no convenient places where they could be bought, even if they had the money with which to buy them. The situation often became critical because of the scarcity, or complete lack, of many things that in more easily accessible areas were classed as necessities. As a result, the region became known as the "land of do-without.")

As we reached beautiful Ekanetlee Gap, the site of our eighth and last camp, there was considerable jollification and some feeble attempts at horseplay. Having been somewhat rejuvenated by the simple food that we obtained from Fondes Cable, we were almost oblivious to the continuing rain.

Hardened by the grueling work of the past eight days, and with a drizzling rain to urge us on, we made the four miles from Ekanetlee to Gregory Bald on Monday morning without a single rest stop and with almost no fatigue, although our rain-soaked packs were still quite heavy. Enveloping clouds denied us most of the fine views, which we had been accustomed to enjoying from the grassy top of Gregory, so we paused but briefly there. Proceeding on to Parsons Bald, only a mile and a half away, and the last peak at the southwest end of the park, we found similar conditions, but we were not in such a hurry to leave as we had been at Gregory. With such a bountiful supply of ripe huckleberries it didn't matter much if the views were blotted out.

Within a half mile of Deals Gap, the goal of our nine days of tramping, we missed our route for the second time of the trip. As before, this was due at least partly to low-hanging clouds and partly to an overgrown trail. It did not concern us very much, however, for our spirits were rising. We were, at long last, on the threshold of victory. Insofar as we knew, or could learn later, we would be the first ever to hike in one continuous trip the whole length of the Great Smokies.

Threats of annihilation had been made against any member of the party who might seek to forge ahead to win the honor of being first to reach Deals Gap. To prevent such impending violence, we lined up, all abreast, and marched triumphantly down into the highway.

Although this was the end of the condensed version of my account of that trip that was published in *American Forests,* it is really not the end of the story.

After making pictures of the bearded and otherwise crusty-looking, weary hikers, our thoughts and efforts were turned to the details of getting back to Knoxville as soon as possible. We knew that we had to make a telephone call to the White Star Bus Lines in Maryville and that the nearest telephone was at Tapoco Lodge, some two miles southward on the highway that passes through Deals Gap. Somehow or other, I do not remember just how, I was designated to make the telephone call and to get to Tapoco the best way I could—even if it be by walking down the highway.

Several cars passed without so much as slowing down—or perhaps they speeded up a bit when they saw the appearance of our crowd. It began to look hopeless, but soon two fishermen passed, slowed a bit, then came to a

Taken August 22, 1932, at the end of the seventy-two-mile hike, in front of the highway construction crew's garage. Our packs still weighed about thirty pounds each. Left to right (with nine days' growth of beard): Charles Cornforth, Charles Gibson, Walter Berry, Guy Frizzell, Harvey Broome, Warner Hall, Carlos Campbell, Carter Whittaker. (Herrick Brown is not pictured. He left us at Buckeye Gap to catch a ride back home.) (Photo by Walter Berry).

stop several feet from the gap. I explained our predicament as best I could, and they somewhat reluctantly picked me up and gave me the desired ride to Tapoco Lodge. After making the call, they even took me back to the gap to await the transportation from Deals Gap to Maryville, where we were to use the regular Maryville-Knoxville bus line back to Knoxville.

Upon arriving in Maryville several minutes before departure time for Knoxville, we went to a nearby drugstore and started to undehydrate ourselves. Never before did ice cream taste so good! Walter Berry even ate a full quart before slowing down. We then entered the bus, before other passengers arrived, and filled the back seats. Within a few minutes other passengers were scattered about in different parts of the bus.

But within a very few minutes the others were crowded as close as possible to the front of the bus, leaving a wide berth between them and us. Surely the odor from our bodies, which had gone nine days without a bath and with little or no change of clothing couldn't have had anything to do with it!!! Perish the thought! We didn't notice anything peculiar about our odors—we had grown accustomed to it very gradually during that nine-day trip. But we did have plenty of room in our part of that bus!

Guy Frizzell and I, who were very close neighbors in Fountain City (then a suburb of Knoxville, but now annexed to the city), somehow got a ride home with another close neighbor, Harry Lawson, for which we were duly thankful. But there was an aftermath. The next morning, when Harry was about to take his daughter to school, she exclaimed: "Dad, what in the world have you been hauling in this car?"

When I then walked into my yard, I was greeted from a distance and told to take a bath and shave off that nine days' growth of beard—just when I was about to become accustomed to the beard! (Little did we know that perhaps we were several years ahead of our time, and that in 1967 we would have been right in style, and a part of "the great unwashed.")

Our return to civilization was gradual, but it was a memorable hike despite all of the hardships we had endured and all the insults that were heaped upon us—especially those from the other occupants of the bus from Maryville to Knoxville.

The nine-day hike of 1932 created so much interest within the Smoky Mountains Hiking Club that a somewhat similar hike was planned for the summer of 1933. Three of the five participants had also made the 1932 expedition. The "veterans" were Walter Berry, Harvey Broome, and Guy Frizzell. Their two new companions were James Freer and Dr. Harold Wiles.

Remembering the difficulties and hardships of the previous long hike, they decided that this one was to be for sheer enjoyment rather than an endurance test. They hiked up the very dim path from Greenbrier to the spring near Mt. Guyot on the first day, then settled down to a lazy pace along the state line to Laurel Top. The descent was down the ridge to Wooly Tops, some two miles below the state line, where the camp was made for the last night, after which they hiked on down to Greenbrier—a total distance of only about twenty-five miles, and only about ten miles of which was along the main crest.

Other club members who were making a one-day hike furnished transportation to the starting point in Greenbrier. The return transportation to Knoxville was provided by a special group that climbed up the steep mountain side and ridge from the Little Laurel Bridge to Wooly Tops, with not even a beaten path to guide us, and camped at Wooly Tops with the long-trippers on their last night out. On the way up, we found an exceptionally large mountain laurel. It measured thirty-five inches in circumference, which is by far the largest that any of us had ever seen.

By way of taking some good news to the long-trip hikers, we took copies of the *Knoxville News-Sentinel,* in which there was a big front-page story announcing the fact that President Franklin D. Roosevelt had just made an allotment of $1,550,000 of federal money with which to "complete" the land purchases for the Great Smoky Mountains National Park. (Members of the park commission could not then know that still another $743,265 was to be needed and gotten.)

Around the Wooly Tops campfire there was a lot of reminiscing about the previous year's long hike as well as reports on the contrasts of the two weeklong outings. It was agreed that those of us who had made the very difficult seventy-two-mile hike were glad that we had done it, but that this year's hike was much more enjoyable.

Although there was no sign of a trail or path between our newly found big mountain laurel and Wooly Tops, we promised to show it to the "veterans" on the trip down the mountain, as none of them had seen such a large specimen. In making that promise, we were forgetting how difficult it is to follow a desired course while going down a ridge (just as in going up a stream on which there are a number of tributaries). It was not long, however, until we realized that we had veered off too far to the left (west), and knew that we had already missed it. Not merely did we miss the big laurel, but we landed in Greenbrier at a point about three miles from our intended destination of Little Laurel Bridge.

At the time of the 1932 and 1933 long hikes the loads that had to be carried were much heavier than would now be necessary for similar hikes. The present chain of trail shelters along the crest of the Smokies had not been built, and tents had to be carried. Furthermore, very few hikers then owned the lightweight, balloon-silk tents, and the heavy pup tents were still used by many hikers. Sleeping bags were owned by very few hikers with the result that many carried heavy woolen blankets in addition to pup tents, cooking equipment, and food. Even though the 1933 trip was much shorter in miles, the men still had to carry supplies for eight days. The younger generation of hikers, with lightweight sleeping bags, little or no need for tents, and with graded trails, are able to make similar hikes with much less effort or hardships.

Those who prefer real wilderness hiking will find many good opportunities between Wooly Tops and various points in Greenbrier.

FOUR IN A PUP TENT

Perhaps most stories should be told in the regular sequence, thus leading up naturally to the climax. Here, however is a story—a true story—that I believe to be more interesting when presented in reverse sequence. Also, as is practiced in television's *Dragnet* series, it is a story where two of the participants must be identified as Miss X and Miss Y—"to protect the innocent."

In 1930 or 1931 Miss Ella Luttrell, secretary of the hiking club, told me, with considerable enthusiasm, that we had "a wonderful new member, a girl from Georgia." In response to my question, Ella told me that her name was "Miss X."

Before I had time to think what I was saying, I gave Ella quite a shock as I said, "Miss X? Why, I've slept with her!"

Now, permit me to back up and tell the first part of the story, which accounted for my tactless remark. In either 1927 or 1928, if I remember correctly, the hiking club conducted a three-day hike up Mt. LeConte. We hiked across the Boulevard Ridge—before the graded trail was built—to the state line, then westward to Newfound Gap and down the road that was being built from Gatlinburg to Newfound Gap. Although we spent the first night in Jack Huff's old balsam-bough lodge, it was necessary for us to carry tents, blankets (that was before sleeping bags were in general use), cooking utensils, an ax, food, and water for use on the second night on Mt. Kephart (then known as Mt. Alexander). As was true with some others, I was carrying a heavy pup tent and two blankets.

With such a heavy load, it was quite a backbreaking task to squirm and sometimes actually crawl through and under the dense tangles of rhododendron that covered the knifelike crest of the ridge. There were not many places where we could walk in an erect position for more than a few yards at a time. Here we learned what the mountain people meant when they referred to growths of rhododendron as "hells." In addition to the difficulties of forcing our way through the shrubs, we had a lot of climbing to do, even though Mt. Kephart is a bit lower than Mt. LeConte. The trail, to use the word loosely, descended steeply for a mile or so, then we had to struggle upward and upward to get to or around the next knob.

When we did finally reach the state line, after another stiff climb, I sought the first convenient place to sit down and rest for a few minutes. I was so near exhaustion that I didn't care much whether I could get up or not. After a few minutes of rest and relaxation, we moved westward a few hundred yards until we found a fairly good campsite—but one without water. After a few more minutes of rest, members of the party—about ten men and the two women—began the preparation of our separate suppers. At the same time, tents were being set up here and there.

Hikers learn many things while making trips into the mountains. It was here, for instance, that Don Crockett learned that when a can of food is to be placed over, or even near, a campfire, it is a good idea to first puncture the top of the can so generated steam can escape. One of Don's cans exploded and splattered corn over most of the hikers.

Also, it was here that I was pleasantly surprised to hear some exceptionally beautiful music. At the sound of the first few notes I supposed that some unknown (to me) species of bird was producing the music. I soon learned, however, that Simon Davis, one of the hikers, gave this thrilling mountaintop concert. He was doing an expert job of whistling a part of the tuneful "William Tell Overture." That composition is always beautiful, in my estimation, but never before had it seemed so enchantingly lovely. I'm sure that the setting on a quiet mountaintop contributed much to my enjoyment late that afternoon. It was, indeed, a musical treat.

As we were completing our supper, with tents already in place, it started to rain, gently at first, then much harder. To my surprise, I noticed that the two girls—Miss X and Miss Y—were just standing around, not even making ready for the night's camping.

"If you will let me have your tent, I'll set it up for you," I volunteered.

Imagine my amazement when they told me that they didn't have a tent. I told them that if they would let me use their ponchos I would let them use my pup tent. I was really flabbergasted when they told me that they didn't have one poncho, much less two. After having lugged that heavy tent and two blankets for two days, especially that torturous second day along Boulevard Ridge, I did not intend to sleep in the rain. Neither did I relish the idea of seeing the girls do so. The only solution I could think of was to lay the matter before the hike leaders, with a suggestion that one of the other men would be assigned to spend the night with the girls and me in my tent. The girls had already accepted the plan, as did the hike leaders and other members of the party. W. W. (Ike) Stanley, a University of Tennessee entomologist, agreed to be the number four occupant of a two-place tent. To say that we slept dry that night is using the word sleep a bit loosely—because we did little sleeping, with all the turning that was involved—but we did keep dry and warm.

I was, of course, recalling those unusual circumstances when I so inadvertently told Ella Luttrell that I had slept with "Miss X."

It's a safe bet that those two girls, who did lots of hiking in later years, never again went on overnight hikes without their own rain gear.

HIKING CLUB ROMANCES

Even in the early years of the Smoky Mountains Hiking Club it became increasingly obvious that the Club was becoming somewhat of a matrimonial bureau. It was not one of the planned activities; it just worked out that way. It is now appropriate to look back to the auspicious beginning of the hiking club romances.

In the spring of 1927 Mrs. Ernest Seaton-Thompson, famous nature writer, was the main speaker for a regional meeting of the Pen Women's Club at Knoxville's Whittle Springs Hotel. Being in the midst of the campaign to establish our national park, it was the practice to seek active support for the park movement from any and all prominent visitors. Accordingly, Col. David C. Chapman invited Mrs. Seaton-Thompson to make a trip into the Smokies. She accepted and agreed to go on a hike to the Chimney Tops with the Smoky Mountains Hiking Club. A condition of her acceptance was that a horse would be provided for her use on that part of the trip from the forks of the road (present location of park headquarters) to the old Indian Gap Hotel, just below the present Chimneys Campground.

At Colonel Chapman's request, I made arrangements for the horse and for an escort of two or three hikers. At the time Brockway Crouch was president of the hiking club and Miss Elsie Wayland was secretary. They, incidentally, had had a few dates. It seemed quite logical, therefore, that Brock and Elsie should be the escorts for the distinguished visitor. When I presented the idea to Brock, he agreed—subject, of course, to Elsie's agreement. So Brock and I went next door to the Bankers Trust Company, where Elsie was working.

As we reached Elsie's desk, which was somewhat secluded on the balcony of the company, I said, "Elsie, we have come to propose to you."

It would be difficult to describe the look of surprise on Elsie's blushing face. The situation soon was relieved when I explained the nature of the "proposal." She readily agreed.

An hour or so prior to the time for Mrs. Seaton-Thompson to arrive, Brock and Elsie got the horse in Gatlinburg and went on up to Andy Huff's sawmill—now the location of park headquarters—and waited for the distinguished visitor. Time for her arrival passed. With only the horse to listen to their conversation, Brock and Elsie waited and waited. In the meantime Hugh White and some of the other hikers had taken Brock's and Elsie's packs on up to the Indian Gap Hotel.

Then, just after the sun had gone down and as the moon was coming over the mountains, Colonel Chapman and Mrs. Seaton-Thompson arrived—not to go on the hike, but to a dinner dance at the Appalachian Club, in Elkmont!

There they were—Brock, Elsie and the horse—a threesome under the light of the full moon. So, they slowly made their way up the long trail. Upon their arrival at the hotel other hikers extended their "sympathy" for the "hardships" that had been imposed upon the club president and secretary. The horse discreetly said nothing.

A few weeks later Brock and Elsie were on another club hike, this one to Mt. LeConte. Next morning Hugh White noticed that Brock had broken club tradition and had shaved—a luxury seldom indulged in by overnight hikers. He passed the word around with the comment that "Brock is really gone this time."

Several years later Brock admitted that it was on the trip, supposedly for Mrs. Ernest Seaton-Thompson, that he and Elsie reached a "general understanding," although the formal engagement did not occur until a bit later. And just six months after that memorable midnight trip they were married. It is a matter of interest that most of the attendants at their wedding were hiking associates. A remark that was heard quite frequently was to the effect that theirs was not merely a wedding, but also a merger of the offices of president and secretary of the hiking club.

Forty years later, as Mrs. Campbell and I were observing our fiftieth wedding anniversary, Brockway obviously recalled my "proposal" to Elsie. In sending orchids for Mrs. Campbell and a carnation boutonniere for me, the flowers were addressed to Mr. and Mrs. Carlos "Cupid" Campbell.

That first hiking club marriage seems to have started a chain reaction. It proved to be the forerunner of a long list of club romances, with a total of forty-five additional marriages during the first thirty-five years of the club's activities. Most of the people involved first met on a club hike, or at some other hiking club activity. Some of the others already were acquainted, but with most of their courting being done on hiking trips. It is doubtful if any of the others had such an unusual development as did Brockway and Elsie, but most of them were interesting in a variety of ways.

Miss Myrtle Seno, secretary of the hiking club, gave this list of the first thirty-four hiking club marriages to me in April 1967. The list follows:

1. Brockway Crouch and Elsie Wayland
2. Kenneth Sanders and Mabel Joyner
3. Parke Brown and Polly Hartman
4. Hugh White and Mary Frank Boone
5. Marshall Wilson and Zelma Tadlock
6. Ernest Fryar and Elsie Zachary
7. Lucien Greene and Dorothy Vance
8. George Hackman and Ruth Aiken
9. Jack Mahaney and Patsy Neal
10. George Morse and Esther Chapman
11. Claude Manning, Jr., and Florence Chapin
12. Herbert Kerr and Shirley Ann Whitney
13. Bill Neal and Charlotte Finnell
14. Jack Craven and Delle Mullen
15. Jack E. Smith and Joan Greenway
16. Franklin O'Dell and Joan Wiley
17. Herrick Brown and Myrtle Graybeal
18. George Vogt and Betty Scott
19. Cole Waggener and Rose Marie Saathoff
20. William Newlin and Lois Ann Inman
21. Jim Lowe and Dotty Argo
22. Addison Hook and Nancy Hale
23. Ed Cox and Christine Scott
24. Eugene Tate and Helen Harvey Meyer
25. Fred H. Sweeton and Phyllis Brown
26. Henri A. Levy and Betty Juresco
27. Harry B. Henry and Elizabeth "Betsy" Johnson
28. Frank Jouvenat and Rosalie Edmondson
29. Fred Behrend and Mary Fern Green
30. Robert W. Holmberg and Reba Justice

31. Oscar Krosnes and Ruby Yarnell
32. John D. Redman and Jean Kincaid
33. Rodney L. Brewster and Nancy Burchfield
34. Gannon Coffey and Amanda Estep

This, mind you, was just the first thirty-five years—and it is safe to guess that the same pattern continued.

LOST IN GREENBRIER

The first night out on a three-day hike from Greenbrier to the state line, my companions—Dutch Roth, G. B. Shivery, and a visitor from North Dakota—and I camped in the orchard of a mountain family.

The next morning, as soon as we completed our breakfast and broke camp, we started our hike on up the mountain, with Mt. Guyot as our main destination. It was the first time any of us had been in that wilderness section of the Smokies. Friends who had been there told us that we would find the ruins of an old cabin between the forks of the creek—the junction of Ramsey Prong and Buck Fork—and "the cherry orchard." But they did not tell us which way to go when we reached the forks of the creek. So at that point we had an important decision to make; would we just take a chance, or would we investigate? We decided to investigate, and Dutch went up the dim trail along or near Buck Fork, as I went up an equally dim path along and near Ramsey Prong. If either or both of us failed to find the cabin, we were to make a mark in the trail to show how far up we had gone.

After going farther than I believed to be indicated, I marked the spot and returned, with no cabin having been found. A few minutes after I got back to where the other two were waiting, Dutch arrived with the information that he had found "the cabin." With this reassurance, we loaded up our packs and started merrily on our way "to Mt. Guyot." For the next few miles we were completely ignorant of any suspicion that we had gone the wrong way, but by late afternoon we became increasingly aware of it and realized that we were lost. The position of the sun enabled us to know that our course was in a general southerly direction whereas we were almost certain that we should have been going toward the east.

Although we knew that we were headed to the main crest at a point some few miles west of Mt. Guyot, we agreed that it was too late to turn back. It would be better to go on up to the top, then turn to the left until we reached our destination. Innocently enough, we assumed that we could still reach Mt. Guyot and get back to our car by, or before, dark. With this in mind we increased our speed somewhat and were soon on the crest, at what we later learned to be Mt. Sequoyah, about 3.5 miles southwest of Mt. Guyot.

With time now becoming quite an important element, we did not pause very long at any point. We were due back in Knoxville that night, and we didn't want our families to think something had happened to us.

The trail from Mt. Guyot down the Tennessee side to Greenbrier was nothing more than a very dim path, used mostly by animals. At times it was difficult to follow, even in daylight, and, alas, the supply of daylight was dwindling too rapidly for our peace of mind. Darkness overtook us when we were down to the general vicinity of Ramsey Cascades, a beauty spot we had never seen or heard of at that time. The old path to Mt. Guyot was some few hundred yards to the north. Down to that point the terrain was relatively free from boulders or other obstructions. But, shortly after dark, we found it impossible to follow the path because we had wandered off just a short distance and were in the midst of an old boulder field, covered with deep beds of moss. Anxious as we were to get back to Knoxville that night, even if it was very late, we were forced to the conclusion that it was not practical, even if possible, to do so.

The more we searched for the dim path, the worse we found the terrain to be. There was not enough room between the boulders for us to make camp, and we could not find a single one that was flat enough, or big enough, for the four of us to sleep on the same rock, so we wound up with two men on one rock and two on another one nearby.

Although we had a little food left, we decided to save it for breakfast. With this chore out of the way the next morning, we scattered out in different directions and began searching for the trail. To our surprise, we had slept, what little we did sleep, less than one hundred yards from the trail.

With the help of daylight, we had very little difficulty in keeping on the trail. In less than an hour, after walking through a grove of huge black cherry trees, we found the remains of an old cabin—the one, incidentally, that was to have been our reassurance that we were on the correct trail. A few hundred yards farther along I found the mark that I had made on the previous day to show where I had turned back.

I have wondered many times what we might have done if both Dutch and I had come back to the forks of the creek with the report that we had both found *the* cabin. But that will have to remain unanswered.

It is interesting to note that all of us had jumped to false conclusions when we had been told about the "cherry orchard." To me, it meant an abandoned fruit orchard that, I assumed, had been planted by the man who had lived in the abandoned cabin. Some years later I learned that the term had been applied to the area, a mile or so below Ramsey Cascades, in which the many big black cherry trees were growing. Many of these trees are from three to four feet in diameter, which is very large for that highly prized forest tree. In prepark days black cherry trees from other parts of the Smokies and surrounding foothills were used for making high-grade furniture.

We did finally get back to Knoxville, but a day late!

About a year later I started back to the Greenbrier wilderness area with an entirely different group—Jim Thompson, Mr. and Mrs. E. Guy Frizzell, Kenneth Sanders, Mabel Joyner, and Harriett Fowlkes. Since I was the only member of the party that had previously been in that part of the Smokies, the others were innocently depending upon me to guide them on the correct route—no trail, mind you—to Mt. Chapman. We had hoped to get most of the way to the state line on the first day. However, we got off to a late start and also lost a little precious time trying to keep on the dim "trail" that we encountered for the first few miles, with the result that we had to make camp before we had much more than gotten started. We hoped to make an early start the next morning, but we were delayed somewhat by the mere increase in numbers in the party. In our plan to get an early start for the second day we were still hoping, blindly, to complete the hike on the second day.

It was, therefore, a bit frustrating when I learned about mid-morning that I had followed the wrong branch as we passed another fork of the creek. I took them up the fork to the right, only to learn a few hours later that we should have gone to the left. In addition, we found some exceptionally rough going, which slowed our pace drastically. The result was that we topped out on Mt. Sequoyah instead of Mt. Chapman, and it was almost dark when we got there. We had no reasonable alternative but to camp there beside the trail, since we knew it would be impossible to go to Mt. Guyot, as had been planned, and still get back to our cars that night. That, of course, meant that we were already unavoidably committed to an extra day more than we had planned to do.

On an earlier hike to Greenbrier Pinnacle, long before the graded trail was built, one of the leaders was Emily Thompson, Jim's daughter. Hikers on that trip started out calling her "Miss Leader." But, when she missed the path that we should have taken, they began calling her "Mis-leader."

Long before we reached the top of Mt. Sequoyah on this second wilderness hike in the Greenbrier area, the other members of the party were calling me "Mis-leader," and for good reason, I guess.

It is doubtful if members of the party now remember very much about that night of camping on Mt. Sequoyah. It is certain, however, that the men still remember the pungent odor that filled the air as we doused the campfire when there was a shortage of water in our canteens.

On the third day we made all the speed we could so that we could get back to Gatlinburg and make telephone calls to our families—families who had expected us back home on the previous day. By early afternoon we had passed the forks of Ramsey Prong and Buck Fork, the starting point of the later graded trail to Greenbrier Pinnacle. A short distance farther along we heard approaching horseback riders, only to learn that it was a search party trying to find us. The late professor S. H. Essary, University of Tennessee botanist and uncle of Guy Frizzell, had organized this party.

It was quite a relief to the girls to be able to ride the remaining few miles, and also a relief for the men to have the horses carry our packs, which were still quite heavy because of the tents and blankets that we had used.

We could not help wondering which way that searching party would have gone if they had not found us before they reached the aforementioned stream junction. If they had taken the left fork—Ramsey Prong—they still would have met us just a little later. But if they had gone up the right fork—Buck Fork—we might have had to send out a search party to hunt for them.

Anyone who does much hiking soon learns that it is extremely difficult to reach a certain point along the main crest by following a stream. There are so many branches or forks of these streams that there are several chances to make the wrong turn. Likewise, it is difficult to reach a certain spot in the foothills when coming down the crest of a ridge because there are equally numerous places where a wrong turn may lead the hiker a few miles away from where he wanted to go. If possible, therefore, it is a good idea—when in unfamiliar territory, where there are no trails—to follow a ridge if going up the mountain, or to follow a stream if coming down.

Shortly after the Appalachian Trail movement was launched, the Smoky Mountains Hiking Club assumed the responsibility for selecting the exact routing through the Great Smokies, and for marking it. We had some interesting experiences on the numerous trail-marking and -measuring trips.

On one occasion Guy Frizzell, Walter Berry, Jesse Bird, and I measured and marked the portion from Newfound Gap eastward to Davenport Gap at the northeast end of the park. Even with about three inches of snow on the ground, we easily completed the trip of thirty-one miles in two days. The one night out was spent beside the trail near the crest of Mt. Chapman. We got the campfire started in a hurry, but it took about thirty minutes to build the fire up to the point where it would keep us warm and enable us to dry our soaked boots. Then, when the fire did get to the point of comfort for us, we decided that we would not need to set up our tents. Instead, we spread our ponchos on the snow, with blankets on the ponchos and with our tent rolls for pillows. We stretched out without any cover over us and were soon asleep—at least, three of us were asleep. By alternating every hour or so, we kept one man awake all night to be sure that the fire did not go out.

Knowing that the ups and downs of a mountain trail can be just as important to a hiker as the mere distances from one point to another, we listed the differences of elevations from each gap to the next summit, then the number of feet of elevation that were lost in descending to the next gap. Insofar as I know, the east half of the Smokies (the thirty-one miles that we measured on that snow-covered trip in 1931) was the first section of the Appalachian Trail for which such helpful information was given. It may even be the only section for which it is given.

On another trail-marking trip, from Dry Sluice Gap to Copper Gap, we reached the starting point by hiking from Greenbrier through Porters Flats to Dry Sluice Gap—at least we intended to top out at Dry Sluice. But the upper portion of the approach route was so badly overgrown because of reduced usage after the building of the graded trail from Newfound Gap that we accidentally veered off to the right and were headed into the barren slopes of Charlies Bunion. We retraced our steps and again found the dim path, only to lose it once more, this time getting off too far to the left. That took us up a slope so steep that when we stopped for a rest we had to hold to some tree or shrub to keep from falling backward down the mountainside.

After we had marked the trail all the way along the crest of the Smokies, we undertook a much harder Appalachian Trail task—that of finding a logical route from the Smokies to Nantahala Gorge, a distance of thirty-five miles; clearing the trail, which we did not have to do in the Smokies, and marking it. Tom DeWine undertook and completed the preliminary search for the best route. He made numerous trips to various points and talked with many nearby residents. This thirty-five-mile route, none of which was familiar to our members, was divided into five sections, and trail-blazing groups were assigned to make the actual determinations and to see if the route was as good as the map studies had indicated.

We camped on the shore of Lake Santeetlah the night before the big exploring trip, during which only temporary marking was done. Before the end of the day we were able to verify the fact that Tom had done a fine job of finding a good route. But that was just the beginning. During the next few years we made a dozen or more work trips, and they really were work trips in every sense of the word. We used bush axes, sometimes called brush axes, for most of the actual clearing. That is a cutting tool with a hooked end that makes it much easier to cut small trees and shrubs. Even with all the hard work, many of the workers found time and energy for a little horseplay now and then. I recall a mock battle in which the ammunition was large acorns from chestnut oaks.

On most of those work trips we would spend the night in the fishing cabins at Deaton's Camp, near Robbinsville, North Carolina. One cold morning we found that some of the car radiators had frozen, but the discovery was not made until we were some distance from the lake. We had to carry so much water that our fingers were nearly frozen.

The trail marking was done by two methods: nailing the official markers to trees along the way; and painting white blazes on numerous other trees. For the painting we first removed the rough part of the outer bark, being careful not to cut into the inner bark. If we made the mistake of cutting too deeply, it meant that new bark would soon grow and cover the blazes; with merely smoothing the bark the white paint would last indefinitely.

We received good cooperation from the landowners, most of whom were big lumber companies. One of these, however, asked that we nail markers

Mary Louise Ogden paints a blaze on the Appalachian Trail, with Evelyn Welch holding the paint, on March 3, 1935. S. A. Ogden looks on to see that it is done properly. Cheoah Bald looms in the left background—so far away, and so elusive.

Snow-covered trail and frost-covered trees between Newfound Gap and the Jump Off. A. G. Roth, Guy Frizzell, and Jesse Bird are the hikers—at the start of a two-day, thirty-one-mile snow hike on November 30, 1935.

Picture of a trail through the fire scald just east of Mt. Buckley. Stone cairns and Appalachian Trail markers on dead or downed trees mark the route, which has a fairly well beaten path under the overhanging weeds, August 26, 1935.

only to small trees, then cut the tree off just above the marker. He explained that this was to prevent some sawmill worker from the danger of getting an eye put out when sawing into a tree with a nail in it.

The Appalachian Trail is a 2,000-mile continuous hiking trail from Mt. Katahdin, Maine, to Springer Mountain in northern Georgia. Even after the entire route was established and marked, there had to be a few relocations made, for various reasons. In the Smokies the route originally went all the way through the park to Deals Gap. It then had to swing several miles back eastward along Yellow Creek Mountain to reach the Cheoah Mountains. This led to a relocation, with the trail leaving the state line at Doe Knob, which is 1.3 miles west of Ekanetlee Gap, then following Twenty-Mile Ridge and Shuckstack down to Fontana Dam, the top of which provides a crossing for the Little Tennessee River, then up to Yellow Creek Mountain.

At another location, many miles from the Great Smokies, it was learned that the route went through property that belonged to a nudist colony and that a camp was soon to be established on it. The owners readily granted permission for the trail to cross their property, but only on the condition that all users would completely disrobe while traversing their property. After a very brief discussion, it was decided to relocate the trail at that point.

Horseback Trips

Having learned the pleasure of seeing the mountains from the back of a good, sure-footed horse while on a longer trip, I started using horses for specially organized groups on trips to Mt. LeConte—especially after I passed age sixty-five, which was in 1957. We used the horses purely for transportation and pack carrying. We never let them go faster than a slow walk. And to prevent getting saddle-sore or from getting stiff knees from riding too long with the knees slightly bent, we would ride for thirty or forty minutes then walk and lead the horses for five or ten minutes.

By this method we were never tired when we reached LeConte Lodge about two o'clock in the afternoon. We always had the horseman send a boy along to take the horses back that afternoon, thus saving one day's horse rent and also saving a stable bill at the lodge. Best of all, however, this left us free to go down by Alum Cave Bluffs the next day.

We also used horses for trips to Gregory Bald and to Thunderhead, riding up from Cades Cove. On these trips we became acquainted with a wonderful horseman, Al Lewis, a former Wyoming cowboy and expert rider. Al did not merely supply us with good horses; he always accompanied us, and from him we learned many interesting things—including bits of outdoor philosophy. On one occasion he furnished the horses and went with us on a fifteen-mile overnight trip across Silers Bald and down Welch Ridge to High Rocks, where we were to spend the night.

That was an interesting but difficult trip, especially the first day's ride. It rained all morning but stopped just before we reached the shelter and spring near the summit of Silers Bald. With the cessation of the rain we anticipated an easy and delightful ride on the remaining seven miles along Welch Ridge. We were under the impression that this part of the trail had been cleared just a few days earlier, but found that no such clearing had been made. And, although the rain had stopped, the wet tree and shrub branches that kept slapping us all afternoon kept us just as wet as if it were still raining. That, however, was not the worst part of the afternoon's ride. The thing that really slowed our progress, and caused a tremendous lot of heavy chopping on the part of Mr. Lewis, was that we encountered more than twenty "blow-downs" that were so big we could neither ride across them nor even find a good detour around them. As a result, Al chopped openings big enough to permit us to pass. He certainly earned more than he received in horse rentals for all of that unexpected trail clearing. It was, therefore, well past mid-afternoon before we reached our destination at the High Rocks fire tower.

The only water available there was from a cistern that stored the water that fell on the fire lookout's cabin. This water, of course, had a taste of cement to it, and the horses would not drink it. One might have expected Al to say, or at least think, "Well, it's there for you. If you don't want it, that is okay with me." But not Al Lewis. He rode his horse and led the other five a distance of four miles down to Forney Creek, where he watered and fed the horses and tethered them so they could graze as much as they wanted during the night. Then he ate his own supper and stretched out on his blanket and slept—knowing that his horses were well cared for.

The next morning he ate his breakfast and fed his horses. Then he watered them again and started back up that four miles to the cabin where we had spent the night. As we rode the fifteen miles back to Tremont, where his horse-carrying truck and our car had been parked, we had the satisfaction of knowing that our faithful mounts at least were not thirsty.

One can learn valuable lessons from almost anyone, but especially from one like Al Lewis.

✐   ✐   ✐

Friends who learned about my occasional horseback trips in the Smokies often asked if it wasn't rather expensive. I never made a direct answer to their inquiries, but responded by some such remark as this:

"I believe you are a football fan, aren't you?"

When, as I knew they would, they admitted that they always bought season tickets, I would follow by asking if they ever went to the out-of-town games that were played by the Vols.

"I never miss one" was the usual reply.

Then, by way of bringing the discussion of "expensive hobbies" to a close, I would ask: "Then, do you want to pursue the subject any further?"

BORROWED PRESTIGE

For more than ten years the Great Smoky Mountains Conservation Association had been trying to get the National Park Service to do the following three things:

1. Clear the underbrush and low tree branches between Little River and the Little River Gorge road so that users of that road could see the natural beauty of the stream.

2. Prevent Cades Cove from reverting to forest as the old settlers moved out after selling their land for park purposes, and to reclear the tree growth that had already started in the earliest farms that were taken out of cultivation.

3. Prevent at least three of the grassy balds from reverting to forest after grazing on those balds was stopped by park regulations.

The reply that we always got was that it was the policy of the Park Service to "let nature take its course." Even with the changing of park administrations the answer was the same, at least until 1945. At that time it was agreed that Cades Cove would be treated as a historic area within a national park. It was also decided that the best method for keeping the meadows open, so as to provide views of the surrounding wall of mountains, was to lease the land to farmers for the grazing of beef cattle. Thus, one of our three objectives was achieved, but with no attending encouragement for the other two projects. It was still a matter of letting nature take its course. Although this, of course, meant that the underbrush between park roads and the immediate adjacent streams became more and more dense, nothing more was done about the problem for another two years.

Early in the summer of 1947 a letter was received from my friend J. Baylor (Joe) Roberts, star photographer for the *National Geographic* magazine. It told that he was soon to make another trip to Tennessee, coming with the *Geographic* vice president and senior writer, Frederick Simpich, to do a story on the Tennessee River. Incidentally, the story was published in the April 1948 issue of *National Geographic,* under the title of "Great Lakes of the South."

Hoping that here was an opportunity to get friend Joe on another Great Smokies trip, I wrote immediately with the suggestion that any story about the Tennessee River must necessarily make reference to the headwater streams, and that the most important of such tributaries was, as he well knew, one of the creeks that originates on majestic Mt. LeConte. I even volunteered to line up some "foreground material" as I had done for him on previous trips to the Smokies. In case you hadn't already guessed it, the "foreground material" meant a couple of pretty girls to be posed in the foreground to add "human interest" to the picture. Joe agreed, with the result that a picture of Miss Jean Cobble and Miss Adele Kennedy, posed in front of beautiful streamside rhododendron just under the footbridge at the start of the Alum Cave Bluffs Trail, was included in the story.

Joe's first trip to the Smokies had been made in 1936, when the Tennessee Conservation Department gave writers and photographers of leading magazines and major newspapers a royal tour of Tennessee. At that time, shortly after the Little River Gorge Road had been widened, there was *no* underbrush between the road and the river. Joe and the others gave high praise to the spectacular beauty of the Little River Gorge Road (Tennessee Highway no. 73). "One of the most beautiful of the entire nation" is the way many of them described it.

On the trip down from Washington to do the Tennessee River story, Joe spent considerable time telling Mr. Simpich about the rare treat that was in store for him when they reached Little River Gorge. It was quite a buildup that Mr. Simpich got—too much, as it turned out. When they finally drove up through the gorge, which was after Joe had made the picture of the pretty girls and rhododendron on the "headwaters" stream; they had a terrible letdown. The underbrush and low-hanging tree branches completely screened off views of the stream for most of the way.

During the following weeks of the Tennessee River trip Joe spent most of his spare time apologizing to Mr. Simpich for what turned out to be a false buildup. As he reported later, he really had "to eat crow." He called from the Knoxville Airport, just before their departure for return to Washington, to tell that the only places where they were able really to see the river was while they were crossing the several bridges. It was obvious that he was a bit angry.

"That is the most fortunate thing that could have happened," I told him.

"The heck you say!!!" was his reply.

I then explained that if he would write me a letter, making sure that it was on *National Geographic* letterhead, I would use the letter in an effort to get some action. I asked him to send me a carbon copy of the letter for my files because I would mail the original, on the same day it was received, to the director of the National Park Service. Joe wrote the letter, as requested, and it was very much to the point. He did not exaggerate; neither did he pull any punches. When I mailed it to National Park Service Director Newton B. Drury I realized that there was no need for comment from me.

As proof that "borrowed prestige" can sometimes accomplish more than years of plodding effort, Great Smokies maintenance crews were at work on the badly needed roadside clearing within a few weeks. Not merely were the underbrush and low tree branches removed, but it was done so carefully, or artistically, that no scars were left. The only evidence was in the ability to see and enjoy the beautiful water while driving through the deep-cut gorge. And it was not just a "one time job." Periodic maintenance has kept the underbrush removed. No trees were cut, and they continued to shade the stream and the road. Similar roadside clearing was done across the mountain along the Oconaluftee River and along other park streams.

Every time I have driven through the picturesque Little River Gorge since Joe Robert's 1947 visit, I recall, with much gratitude, that it was the help given by him that made it possible to get the needed roadside clearing. Moreover, I find myself wishing that all the throngs of people that enjoy that trip each year could know and appreciate the debt of gratitude we all owe to him and *National Geographic* for their "borrowed prestige."

In addition to the 1936 trip as guest of the Tennessee Conservation Department, Mr. Roberts made at least three other trips to the Great Smokies. It was my pleasure to take him to see, and photograph, the large beds of white-fringed phacelia above Elkmont, and to take him on another trip through Little River Gorge and to Laurel Falls for pictures of the many kinds of wildflowers as well as on a snowstorm trip to Mt. LeConte. I furnished "foreground material" for those trips, too. On the LeConte trip we spent the night, then hiked almost a mile to Myrtle Point the next morning to see a glorious sunrise. In describing the sunrise trip, for which the temperature was nine degrees above zero, Joe said: "This is what I'd call suffering for art's sake."

While waiting for lunch at LeConte Lodge, we saw a phenomenon that was new to all of us—a complete circle "rainbow" almost straight overhead. Joe told us, however, that airplane pilots who are flying very high often see such "rainbows" below them.

Before starting his long years of work for *National Geographic,* Joe was a sports photographer. On one of our trips I asked him to compare the two radically different types of photography, especially asking which he really liked best.

"I'll answer that with another question," he said. "Which would you rather be, a justice of the peace, or a member of the United States Supreme Court?"

He did, however, explain that while he was in the sports field, a picture he had made at a baseball or football game would be in the paper on the same afternoon—and usually forgotten before the next afternoon. At the *Geographic,* while his pictures seldom reached the printed pages until months later, many of them were kept for many years by millions of readers.

National Geographic magazine gave a reception for Mr. Roberts on March 31, 1967, at the time of his retirement.

CONFUSING NAMES

Confusion in the nomenclature of the Great Smokies was not—and is not—limited to the former duplications such as peaks and streams bearing the same names, most of which were eliminated by the work of the bistate nomenclature committees. There can also be confusion about the names of plants and other things as is shown in the following incidents.

A friend was taking his wife on a motor trip to the Smokies at a time when there was an abundance of Hercules Club, or Devil's Walkingstick (*Aralia spinosa*) in bloom. The wife, a flower lover who was not familiar with this rank-growing shrub, asked, "Why can't our Nandinas grow that tall?"

Perhaps very few people confuse Hercules Club with Nandinas, but a large number do get confused, and badly so, with other plants. It is my guess that a majority of nonbotanists who go to the Smokies think of all the conifers—hemlocks; which many mountain people call spruce pines; red spruces; and the Fraser firs or balsams—as pines. I have heard it so many times that I have stopped being surprised. And many people, especially those living in the mountains or foothills, refer to rhododendrons as laurel and to the laurel as ivy.

It gets to be somewhat amusing when we hear some of the names by which the mountain people knew some of the plants. Laura Thornburg, author of the delightful book *The Great Smoky Mountains*, for many years spent most of her summers in her Gatlinburg cottage and heard so many different names for "hearts-a-burstin'" (*Euonymus americanus*) that she started carrying a sprig of the shrub around with her as she asked one and all if they could identify the plant for her—as though she didn't already know it.

Within a few weeks she had about twenty names for it. In addition to "hearts-a-burstin'," the names heard most often were strawberry bush, arrowwood, spindle bush, and wahoo, and there were many others that were not quite so descriptive of the plant or the attractive and oddly colored fruits. One other, however, came into rather general use in certain circles. One man, who kept a straight face, told her that the real name was "Kiss me and I'll tell you."

Hiking club members refused to use any other name for the next several years. They often had a little fun at the expense of visitors by using that name. One of the women would be carrying a sprig, with the ripe fruits on it, as other members managed to get an unsuspecting visitor to ask her the name of the plant. On a certain trip, Willa Love Galyon, the club secretary at the time, was carrying the fruits. Dr. Frank Bohn, a scientist from New York, was led into asking the name, after which he was told to ask Miss Galyon, who was carrying it, which he did.

"Kiss me and I'll tell you," she replied.

"Now, what is the name?" he asked as he kissed her, thus feeling that he had qualified.

"Kiss me and I'll tell you," Miss Galyon again told him.

By that time he was beginning to understand that she had already told him—twice!

⊘ ⊘ ⊘

Despite the fact that it required us to drive twice as far to reach the starting point of our hikes, we made occasional jaunts to Heintooga Overlook, Hemphill Bald, and the Cataloochee area. Heintooga was also where we could find an occasional staurolite—a naturally formed six-sided prismatic crystal—sometimes known as "fairy stone crosses" and sometimes just "fairy crosses."

In the prepark years we reached Heintooga by driving across through Newfound Gap to Cherokee and thence eastward to Maggie Valley. This part of the drive was over fairly good roads, but from there to Black Camp Gap we had to use a narrow, crooked, and steep road. Heintooga was the favorite because it provided wide, sweeping panoramas of the main crest of the Smokies all the way from Clingmans Dome to Mt. Guyot. The absence of steep cliffs dropping off below Heintooga kept it from being a rival for Mt. LeConte as a vantage point.

About a mile of the trail was along or near Flat Creek, which provided the water for beautiful Flat Creek Falls just a short distance farther downstream. Another interesting feature of this creek is that it is only a few hundred feet lower than the crest of Heintooga Ridge, which runs parallel to the stream. Shortly before the trail crossed Flat Creek it passed through a small field in which the grass was only a few inches tall, as a result of grazing. The short grass made it possible for us to find the occasional staurolite. My total find, in three early hikes to Heintooga Overlook, was only five or six of those naturally formed six-sided prismatic crystals. These unusual minerals are often "twinned" so as to resemble a cross or an X.

Although a cross-section of these crystals has six sides, they are not hexagonal because two of the six sides are wider than the other four sides, thus producing angles of different degrees and producing a stem that is wider than the thickness.

Staurolites are found in very few locations, and those are small and widely scattered. In some parts of the country nature has formed them actually in the shape of crosses, with the combined stems crossing each other at right angles. The few that were found beside the trail near Flat Creek, however, were irregular in shape, and were more like the letter X. The crossing stems are about twice the size of a wooden matchstick. Those that I found, and others from Flat Creek that I have seen, were from only an inch to an inch-and-a-half in length. In some other areas the length may be up to three inches. Where they are found in sufficient quantities, they are attached to small silver or gold chains and sold as items of jewelry. This was not the case at the Flat Creek site, however, because they were so irregular in shape and so few of them were found there.

Even so, the few of us who did find a staurolite while on a hike to Heintooga Overlook considered it as a lucky bonus for a good hike.

With visitors, and to a certain extent with local people, there remains some confusion in the names of the four major streams on the Tennessee side, and at the ends of the park, and with the various branches or prongs of two of these streams. One or both of two words—"pigeon" and "little"—appear in all of these names. Near the eastern end of the park the principal stream is the *Pigeon River,* sometimes erroneously called the Big Pigeon, to distinguish it from another stream. The next streams to the west are the three prongs of *Little Pigeon River.* The East Prong of Little Pigeon River drains the Jones Cove section of Sevier County. The Middle Prong of Little Pigeon River flows from the Greenbrier and Emerts Cove areas. The West Prong of Little Pigeon River drains the Gatlinburg and Mt. LeConte areas. The three prongs meet at the north (lower) edge of Sevierville.

The third of the four streams is *Little River,* with its three prongs. The East Prong of Little River flows from the Elkmont section of the Smokies, draining everything from Sugarland Mountain to Miry Ridge. The Middle Prong of Little River provides the drainage of the Tremont area, from Miry Ridge to Defeat Ridge. The West Prong of Little River carries the runoff from the area between Defeat Ridge and Bote Mountain. The larger stream at the western end of the park is the *Little Tennessee River.* The part of this stream that is along or near the park border is, however, no longer a "river," but a series of lakes formed by power dams—Fontana Lake, Cheoah Lake, Calderwood Lake, and Chilhowee Lake.

Low places along the main crest of the Smokies also provide some little bit of confusion for visitors, especially those from the western mountains and from New England. Here those low places are designated as "gaps." In the west they are "passes," and in New England they are "notches."

Where is Indian Gap? There was a time, long before the Great Smokies became a national park, when there was a little confusion on that point. About 1930 Marshall Wilson and I spent a day in Emerts Cove and Greenbrier in an effort to learn something of the early history of that part of the Great Smokies foothills. Although we talked with a number of "old-timers," "Uncle" Noah Ogle, a lifelong resident of Emerts Cove, gave our best information.

In response to our question, Mr. Ogle told us that the early settlers of that community had come over from North Carolina. On further questioning he told that they had crossed the Smokies at "Indian Gap." At this point it is important to establish the fact that the place currently designated as Indian Gap is a mile and a half west of Newfound Gap, and approximately ten miles west of the gap nearest to Greenbrier and Emerts Cove.

"By what route did they come over from Gatlinburg?" I asked.

"They didn't come through Gatlinburg," he replied.

I then asked how, by what route, they could come from Indian Gap to Greenbrier without coming through Gatlinburg—which, incidentally, was known as White Oak Flats during pioneer days.

"They just came on down through Porters Flats," he explained.

That told us that his "Indian Gap" was, at the time of our visit, known as Dry Sluice Gap, just east of Charlies Bunion. It also caused us to wonder if there may not have been a number of "Indian Gaps" along the crest of the Smokies—the gap through which Indians had crossed during their trips into the various foothills communities on the Tennessee side of the mountain.

"Uncle" Noah Ogle also told us that "Fitified Spring," beside the trail between the Greenbrier and Trillium Gap, had been so named after the spring started having "fits." Prior to a mild earthquake in 1912 that spring flowed naturally, but the earthquake caused the shifting of rocks and created a siphon action in the underground supply stream, thus producing the intermittent or "fitified" flow of the spring.

Several mountain peaks and other features were named for men who had been prominently identified in some way with the Great Smokies or with the park movement. A considerable amount of history has been recorded or recognized by this practice. A few of the major peaks that were named in this manner are Clingmans Dome, Mt. Guyot, Mt. LeConte, Mt. Chapman, Mt. Sequoyah, Mt. Kephart, Mt. Cammerer, and Gregory Bald.

A great many other peaks, ridges, gaps, and streams were given descriptive names. To people living just below the abrupt end of a high ridge, where they can't see the sides of the ridge, the terminus looms up as though it was a huge cone. Several such ridge-ends were given the name of Round Top. Thus, if Mt. LeConte had been named by the people living in or near Tuckaleechee Cove, the location of Townsend, it is likely that the name would have been Round Top. Although the summit of LeConte is approximately a mile long, it appears to be conical in shape when seen from Townsend, which is about sixteen airline miles west of LeConte.

A peak or a stream with dense growths of mountain laurel was likely to wind up with the name of Laurel Top or Laurel Creek. Streams on which primitive gristmills were located were often known as Mill Creek. Since each separate community did the naming of features near them, it is understandable that there were so many duplications of these descriptive names.

The proximity of the nearby Cherokee Indian reservation caused the use of several Indian names, especially during the period when nomenclature committees set out to eliminate the use of so many duplicate, and therefore confusing, names.

Not all of the Indian-sounding names have such an origin, however. At least two such names are entirely synthetic—not Indian. I've heard comments about the "beautiful Indian name" of Tapoco, the resort and power village in North Carolina near where the Cheoah River flows into the Little Tennessee River and just below the Cheoah Dam. The name Tapoco was coined by using the first two letters of each one of the three-word names of the Aluminum Company's subsidiary, the Tallassee Power Company. Yes, Tapoco does sound like a good Indian name, doesn't it?

The other peak with "the beautiful Indian name" was Mt. Lumadaha. Before the tent-shaped peak on the state line near Mt. Guyot was officially designated as Mt. Chapman, it had no generally recognized name. The synthetic name of Lumadaha came into use for a short time, following a hike to that peak by Lucien Greene, Marshall Wilson, Dave Huffine, and Harvey Broome. The coined name of Lumadaha was created by using the first two letters of the quartet's first names—<u>Lu</u>cien, <u>Ma</u>rshall, <u>Da</u>ve, and <u>Ha</u>rvey.

When that trip was planned, I was to have been a member of the party, but I had to drop out because of sickness in my family. I've often wondered what the short-lived name might have been if I had also made the hike with them.

An element of mystery is suggested by some of the picturesque place-names of the Great Smokies.

One of these, Huggins Hell, is applied to the extremely rugged gorge that extends from Alum Cave Creek up to Myrtle Point of Mt. LeConte. The very name itself adds a touch of glamour. How did it get such a name? Legend—pure fiction, no doubt—tells that a man by the name of Huggins had become interested in the area and told friends that he was going to explore it. He was told that he would never find his way out if he went into it. He is said to have replied that he would go through and come out on the other side, or he would go to hell while trying. Since he was not seen again, the region became known as Huggins Hell.

There are so many unique and interesting names in use that Paul M. Fink, veteran Great Smokies enthusiast of Jonesboro, Tennessee, has made a special study of the names of park peaks, ridges, gaps, and streams, and the sources of those names. He has published a delightful and informative book with the title of *That's Why They Call It . . .* That book lists and gives the origins of, and reasons for, such unique and picturesque place names as Bote Mountain, Defeat Ridge, the Boulevard, Charlies Bunion, Wooly Top, and many others.

Many of Jim Thompson's early pictures of the Smokies had their names placed on the negatives so each print could easily be identified. One of these pictures, made from Myrtle Point, was labeled as Huggins Hell. Girls working in the photographic printing room were checking out the prints made for the day. As they picked up each print they would read off the name. "Huggins Hell," one of them read off. "Who said so?" the other asked.

✑   ✑   ✑

From the earliest days of the hiking club considerable interest was shown in the Huggins Hell area. Except for a few fishermen who had fished its lower edge, they had never heard of any person who had penetrated the region. So, in the summer of 1927 members of the club planned an exploring trip for which three days were set aside. Members of the party were Dr. H. M. Jennison, A. G. "Dutch" Roth, Harvey Broome, Lucien Greene, Ted Sizemore, and Carlos C. Campbell. Ted, who had not done any mountain hiking, was wearing oxfords when he joined the others in Knoxville. He was told that he should have hiking boots since we were going into very rough country. "All I want is a mountain to climb" was his reply, and he insisted to go on without boots.

On the first day we carried our heavy packs to the top of Mt. LeConte. Since we knew almost nothing of the route we were to follow, we allowed two days for the trip down through Huggins Hell. Our packs, containing pup tents, food, and cooking utensils for use on the second night out, were quite heavy. Even so, the going was rather easy for a short distance after we left Myrtle Point. But the farther we went, the more difficult it became. At first there was no stream, of course, but we soon came to a small one. Then, as other small branches joined from both sides, it became a sizeable stream. At times it was easier to walk, or hop from rock to rock, right down the streambed. When the going was too bad there, we would take to the banks, but before long we invariably ran into tangles of rhododendron that sent us back to our rock hopping. We alternated many times between the increasingly large stream and the rhododendron-lined banks. This meant that the going was quite slow.

There was a great deal of uncertainty and anxiety in the minds of the hikers. And for Ted Sizemore, it became quite a psychological strain, since it was all new to him. Although he was the largest and by far the strongest man in the group—at the time he was the YMCA heavyweight wrestling champion for the entire south—he began to grow weary, more from worry than from physical strain. This condition rapidly worsened, and he was threatening to just give up. In an effort to ease the situation, Dutch Roth took Ted's pack and carried it in addition to his own heavy pack. Although none of the others were in a similar condition, we were all getting a bit tired, and we began to think about where and when we would camp for the night, although it was not yet mid-afternoon. Really suitable campsites were nonexistent, but we kept looking as we trudged wearily on down the creek. This stream, flowing through Mr. Huggin's hell, has been officially named Styx Branch.

Then, when we were least expecting it, we found the dim path made by trout fishermen. All of a sudden, Ted forgot all about being tired, much less exhausted, and he again took over the carrying of his own pack—thus proving that his problem had stemmed from uncertainty and worry rather than from physical exertion. But he was not the only one who was somewhat revived by seeing even the dim signs of civilization.

The fisherman's trail that we found was somewhere in the vicinity of what we now know as Arch Rock. Although we passed within ten or twenty feet of this "hole through the ridge," we did not even see it. In fact, we had not then so much as heard that there was such a place—now a landmark on the Alum Cave Trail to Mt. LeConte.

From there on down we made much better time, and in a few more minutes we reached what was then known as Grassy Patch, but later changed to Alum Cave Parking Area. Shortly after mid-afternoon we reached the former Indian Gap Hotel, just below the present Chimneys Campground. Thus, we had done in less than one day what we had feared would take at least two hard days. We were later to learn that Roaring Fork Creek, on the opposite side of Mt. LeConte, is even rougher and more precipitous than the Huggins Hell area.

After a good night's rest at the hotel, we made an extra hike the next day, just for exercise, as we told friends. On this, the third and last day of our trip, we made the roundtrip hike along the beautiful Road Prong trail to Indian Gap.

Mountain hiking and motoring gives some excellent opportunities to observe surprising examples of perspective.

From a number of points, Cliff Top—the sunset point of Mt. LeConte, appears to be higher or taller than the actual high top—but the elevation of Cliff Top is only 6,555 feet above sea level whereas the high peak has an elevation of 6,593 feet—or 38 feet higher than Cliff Top. And from the Newfound Gap Highway (U.S. 441) about two to three miles up from park headquarters, Balsam Point—the western end of LeConte, appears to be the highest point, although it has an elevation of only 5,450 feet, thus is actually 1,143 feet lower than the high peak.

Another good illustration of deceptive perspective is seen at Chimney Tops. Viewing from the vicinity of Chimneys Campground, one would find it hard to believe that the south peak, at the right, is actually about 50 feet higher than the sharp left peak. But a view from the vicinity of the Loop Over or Bear Pen Hollow shows the true relationship.

Chimney Tops as seen from the Newfound Gap Highway at Bear Pen Hollow (just above the Loop-Over), May 26, 1934.

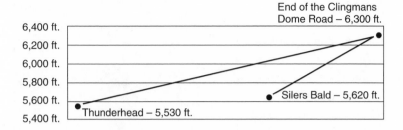

Relative heights of Thunderhead, Silers Bald, and the end of Clingmans Dome Road

A rather dramatic example of deceptive elevations is provided when looking westward from the end of Clingmans Dome Road. From that vantage point, on a clear day, one looks down on Silers Bald about four miles, airline, to the west. Then, considerably higher on the horizon, Thunderhead is seen, some 11 air miles from the end of the road. On many occasions I have pointed out these two peaks for the benefit of strangers. Usually I tell the elevation of one of these well-known points, then ask the stranger to guess the elevation of the other peak.

Without exception, the guesses have been that Thunderhead is the higher peak, with many of them guessing it to be as much as 200 to 300 feet higher than Silers Bald.

The surprising fact, to the guessers, is that the elevation of Thunderhead is 5,530 feet above sea level, whereas Silers Bald is 5,620 feet elevation, thus 90 feet higher than Thunderhead. The main factor that contributes to the deceptive appearances is the fact that the viewing is done from an elevation of approximately 6,300 feet, at the edge of the road's end, which enables the viewer to look down on both peaks. If they were being seen from some point more nearly the same elevation, Thunderhead would not appear to be the higher peak. Without taking this factor into consideration, it is difficult for visitors to believe that Thunderhead is lower than Silers Bald. It requires a close look at the foregoing sketch to appreciate fully the significance of the relative elevations of Thunderhead and Silers Bald.

What is it?

How tall is it?

The subject of this picture, sometimes mistaken for a huge cross, illustrates a different type of deceptive perspective. I have shown enlargements of a picture of this to many friends with a request that they guess how tall it is. Very few guessed less than ten feet, with a majority of estimates ranging from fifteen to fifty feet.

Until I showed a summertime picture of the same "structure," some of the guessers found it difficult to realize that the picture shows a frost-covered trail sign. Without the beautiful covering of hoarfrost the sign points the way to a nearby

What is this frost-covered "structure" near the end of Clingmans Dome Road?

comfort station. This winter view was made to appear deceptively tall by placing the camera at ground level and shooting upward.

This location of the trail sign, about four feet tall, is at the end of Clingmans Dome Road. Continuous winds caused the hoarfrost to form only on the windward side. The "fingers of ice" are from three to four inches long. Just a few hundred yards up the trail toward the tower, the dense forest subdues the winds with the result that hoarfrost forms on all sides of every twig or other object when clouds are down on the mountain during freezing weather.

✍   ✍   ✍

Hikers learn very quickly that the various mountains of the Great Smokies are, indeed, very rough and rugged. They soon learn, often with sore muscles as a lingering reminder, that the so-called laurel slicks of the Smokies are far from being "slick" and that "laurel hells" make a much more accurate or descriptive name for what the botanists know as "heath balds."

To fliers and airplane passengers, however, it is quite a different story. Those rugged peaks and ridges, with almost precipitous cliffs, appear to flatten out when viewed from the air. Lucien Greene and I were much surprised at that fact when, in 1926, we spent two hours flying over the Smokies with Frank Andre as the pilot. The craft, then considered modern, was a Waco biplane with an open cockpit. Lucien and I sat in the front seat, with Frank operating from the pilot's regular seat just back of us.

Although the speed was very slow by 1967 standards, we faced so much wind that we had to wear helmets to protect us from both the noise and the wind.

Our takeoff was from the Knoxville "airport" then located on Sutherland Avenue near where West High School was later built. We flew over Maryville to Gregory Bald, which we circled twice, then headed up the state line range to Thunderhead, which we also circled twice. Our course then left the main range to our right as we headed straight to majestic Mt. LeConte, which we circled three or four times so we could get better views of our favorite peak. Then we made a beeline for Mt. Guyot, flying high above the Greenbrier wilderness area, for a good look at that second-highest peak of the Smokies. We had been flying about two thousand feet above the various peaks, but as we left Mt. Guyot, we started losing elevation rather rapidly so we could get a good broadside view of Mt. LeConte from a semi-close-up position. It was not until we were looking upward toward the summit of LeConte that the Smokies again began to look like what we knew them to be. Our trip over the Smokies lasted for two full hours, much of which was used in circling the peaks.

The flattening-out effect of seeing the mountains from a considerable distance above is closely related to the fact that in making embossed or relief maps it is necessary to use a totally different scale for the vertical measurements than the scale used for the horizontal distances. Most relief maps use a three-to-one, or at least a two-to-one, vertical exaggeration. If the same scale were used for both, it would give the maps the appearance of the mountains as when one sees them from a high-flying airplane.

Tourists

During the first year or two of the ten-year struggle to get a national park in the Great Smokies, I was a bit resentful when I heard anyone refer to the attractiveness of the other national parks. It took that much time for me to fully realize or recognize the fact that each and every national park is superlative in some particular respect. I didn't have to yield any of my enthusiasm for the Great Smokies when I accepted that fact.

We began to see more and more visitors from the western states that have one or more national parks. I began to make it a practice to approach the occupants of cars from those states and tell them that I was glad to know that they have some outstanding parks in their own states. *Without exception,* the replies were something like this:

"Yes, but we don't have the beautiful green-clad mountains that you have here in such abundance."

Most of the visitors from other states make a lot of pictures during their Great Smokies trips. When I see a man making pictures with other members of his family in the foreground, I make a practice of offering to snap the picture for him, thus giving him the privilege of getting in the picture— "so you can prove that you, too, were here." A majority of them accepted my offer and expressed appreciation for it.

All too often, the visitor has his wife and/or other members of the party lined up beside their own car, with the car as the principal background. In such cases I suggested that they line up differently so that the picture can also show some mountains as the background. They usually agreed that such was a good idea.

This recalls the fact that some wit has said that "A tourist is a person who drives five hundred miles to get a picture of his wife standing by his car."

PHOTOGRAPHY

Many of photographer Jim Thompson's earliest pictures of the Great Smokies were made on trips of the Smoky Mountains Hiking Club. Since photographic equipment in those days was quite heavy, it became a practice of other hikers to offer assistance to Jim. One member would carry the tripod. Another would carry a case of film holders.

This worked well at first; but in the course of time, when Jim saw a good picture subject, he couldn't make the desired picture because one or another of his volunteer "helpers" would be on ahead, out of sight. Jim soon noticed that I was usually the only one who stayed with him. This soon caused Jim, in self-defense, to decline help from any other volunteers, and I became his only helper. I didn't object to this, because I found him to be good company and I enjoyed watching the way he went about the details of picture making.

It became increasingly obvious that group hiking and picture making had many disadvantages. In the first place, when we stopped to make a picture, most of the group went on ahead, with the result that the big group was soon split up into two or more smaller groups. Another objection was that when Jim wanted a *few* people in the picture most all of the group wanted in. Not merely that, but too many of them insisted on posing—looking at the camera instead of looking into the scene. Still another problem was that many of them, although dressed suitably for hiking, were not dressed for picture making.

Jim and I then turned gradually to specially planned picture-making trips, with selected people to do the posing. They understood that we were starting *toward* a certain objective but that the primary purpose was to make pictures wherever suitable subjects were found. We usually reached the intended goal, but occasionally we spent so much time along the way that we didn't even get to the top of the mountain that we were climbing.

This hiking/picture-making association with Jim continued, with varying degrees of activity, for more than ten years. At no time during that period did I feel even the slightest interest in taking up photography as a hobby. And never once did I make any conscious effort to study the techniques that Jim used.

Then, in 1935, I won an inexpensive folding camera in some sort of slogan-writing contest, and almost before I knew it, I was becoming an amateur photographer. As I made preparations for any picture that I was making, I found that I was drawing heavily from information, especially on composition, that I had more or less absorbed while watching Jim at work. In retrospect, I realize that I had been learning a basic difference between snapshots and photographs.

Here is a good illustration. In the early park days, the road from Pigeon Forge to Gatlinburg was mostly along the western side of the river. There was an interesting mountain home, covered with split boards, or "shakes," near the north end of the present tunnel. It was reached by crossing a swinging footbridge. Many times, as we passed this spot, we would agree that this was a picture that we just must make sometime. It soon became one of the most urgent pictures on our "must list." Finally, it became the "mustiest" subject on the list.

Pretty soon we made time for this special picture. Jim parked his car so it would not be in the way and began to explore for the best spot from which to make it. With the big camera in place on his best tripod, he put the focusing cloth over his head and studied the subject. From the first spot, between the road and the river, there was some objectionable material either in the foreground or background. He moved a few feet upstream and looked again, only to move twice more before moving to the opposite side of the road. There, again, was always something that would have detracted from the natural beauty and interest.

Incidentally, one can stand and look at an object such as this cabin and completely ignore undesirable objects, but not so in a picture. A pile of rubbish in the foreground would become the dominant feature in a picture, although it would be scarcely, if at all, noticed in on-the-spot viewing.

Having exhausted the possibilities on both sides of the roadway, we went back down the road several yards and climbed the bank above the road shoulder. At the third test spot Jim found just about what he had been seeking, so he made two or three shots, on 8 x 10 film.

During the months that Jim and I had been making vague plans to get a picture of that swinging bridge and cabin, we had seen a number of people stop, roll down the car window, snap a picture, and move on, with the lapse of only a minute or two. What they got were "snapshots." Jim, on the other hand, produced a definitely artistic "photograph." It was used on a full page in the August 1936 issue of *National Geographic*. The head of the photographic section of the *Geographic* liked it so much that he asked Jim for the loan of the negative so he could make a huge enlargement for use on the wall of his office. Although a photographer usually does not like to let others use his negatives, it is understandable that this was a happy exception.

As I began to make pictures during my Great Smokies trips, often still with Jim, I supposed that I would exhaust the possibilities when my collection reached two hundred in number. But in less than five years the number had reached more than thirty-five hundred black-and-white pictures. More than half of those had been published in magazines, major newspapers, and books and as postcards. Later, I made a few thousand 35mm color pictures and an equal number of stereo slides, also in color.

Long before that time I realized that during all those years with Jim I actually had been taking an intensive course in photography, and from an expert. Many times, in thinking about my photographic experiences, I recalled having read or heard a statement attributed to President James A. Garfield, that "The ideal college is a log, with a student at one end and Mark Hopkins (a renowned educator and theologian of the day) on the other end." In my case, Jim Thompson was the Mark Hopkins and I, without realizing it at the time, was the student.

Early in my picture-making activities, I learned that editors to whom I submitted pictures, usually along with an article about the Great Smokies, had definite ideas about what they would accept. On several occasions I was told that a certain picture would be acceptable only if it were horizontal in proportions; at other times it had to be vertical. Or they would like it if it had some people in it—or, perhaps, if it did not have people. This led me to make many of my subjects both shapes, as well as with and without people. Almost invariably I would send at least twice as many pictures as had been requested. This frequently led to the use of a larger number than had been mentioned in the original request.

Preconceived Opinions

Many, perhaps most, of the erroneous statements about people who live in our southern mountains seem to be based on preconceived notions which the visiting writers brought with them, rather than on what they saw or heard while in these mountains.

I observed a clear case of this when I took a northerner on a trip to Cades Cove, where he wanted to see how the people lived. Our route was across the old Rich Mountain Road because the present road up Laurel Creek had not been built. As we drove around the many hairpin curves on the north side of Rich Mountain, we came to a new cabin that had been built just a few months earlier. It was a rather crude one-room home, made of perpendicularly placed rough lumber.

On one side was a door and on the other side there was an opening about two feet square, but without glass, that served as a window. There were no openings in the other two sides. The rough boards had never been painted.

The building was, apparently, just about what he had expected to find, and he asked that I make a picture of it for him. When I showed an enlarged print to him several days later he was almost angry. "That is not what I wanted," he exclaimed.

I soon learned that what he was really objecting to was that the picture also showed the beautiful flowers that were growing in front and at the sides of that simple house. They made it a rather attractive picture because the camera could not ignore or omit the flowers, as he obviously had done while looking at the more-or-less crude building.

"I didn't plant the flowers, I merely photographed them," I replied, "It is easy to see that it is the home of a poor family, but as you can see, they do have an appreciation for beauty despite their poverty." Incidentally, the homes in Cades Cove were much too nice and neat to be of interest to him. He didn't ask for pictures of any of them.

⚘   ⚘   ⚘

Another—though this time humorous—case of a "preconceived opinion" was in 1935, when the winds of change seemed to presage a whole new way of life for the mountain people. I made a trip around the western end of the Smokies and on through North Carolina's Nantahala Gorge. It was on an early summer day, and many mountain farmers were busily cultivating their hilly cornfields.

A short distance from the gorge I was intrigued by a rustic sight that caught my eye. A farmer was plowing his cornfield, with a team of oxen providing the "horse-power." That, of course, called for a picture and I found the farmer to be coop-erative. At my request, a little boy, dressed in coveralls, also got into the picture.

When I showed the pic-ture to George F. Barber, physical director of the Knoxville YMCA and the first president of the Smoky Mountains Hiking Club, he shook his head and said: "My, my! I wonder what the future holds for that little fel-low!"

"That's what I'm worry-ing about, too," I replied.

To this George said he couldn't see why I should be worrying about the future of the little boy.

"Because he is my son, Jim," I explained.

This is the first year these oxen have been worked. T. J. Ledbetter, of Almond, North Carolina, with Jimmy Campbell as a visitor, May 1, 1934. This is beside Highway US 19, near the North Carolina border of the park.

In the summer of 1936 at Big Meadows, President Franklin D. Roosevelt dedicated the Shenandoah National Park. It is possible that a conversation I had with him that day had a bearing on his first visit to the Smokies the following year.

Though I was not actually introduced to the president at the Shenandoah dedication, I did get some excellent pictures of him, specially posed, just before he entered the speakers stand—by way of a ramp at the rear. In fact, he kept granting my requests for "another shot" until he was a few minutes late in reaching the speakers stand. Despite that fact, his attitude was such that one might have thought the purpose of that visit was to let those pictures be made. Never once did he give any indication of impatience. The Secret Service men, however, began to show some concern.

Later, just after the dedication, I was standing near his car for several minutes while Mrs. Roosevelt was holding a press conference in a nearby tent. During most of that time I watched and listened as several senators and other dignitaries brought their children or friends to meet the president. During a lull in this activity, I spoke to Mr. Roosevelt, reminding him that Great Smokies enthusiasts appreciated the many things he had done to help get our park established. And I told him that we were hoping that he might soon visit the Smokies and see for himself what he had helped to create.

He expressed interest, but added that on his next trip to Tennessee he would be going to Chattanooga. I then reminded him that a trip to the Smokies could be made at the same time—that our park was almost directly on the way to Chattanooga. He did not make further comment about the possibility of visiting the Smokies, but within a few months we learned—before the public announcement—that the visit was to be made in June 1937.

When an important visitor is coming to the Smokies, we always hope for "good" weather, and at the time of the visits made by members of the secretary of the interior's works committee (they later recommended the Great Smokies as being worthy of becoming an important national park), the weather cooperated beautifully.

But at the time of President Franklin D. Roosevelt's first visit, in the summer of 1937, it was a different story. During the drive from Gatlinburg to the end of Clingmans Dome Road, it was quite cloudy, but did not rain.

President Roosevelt paused, after getting out of his car, to permit amateur photographers to get a few more "shots" just prior to the dedication of Shenandoah National Park on July 3, 1936.

Then, while prepared lunches were being eaten at the end of the road, the clouds opened, and most of us were soon soaked to the skin.

The president was seated in a touring car, with the top raised for his protection while he ate his lunch. U.S. senators and other dignitaries—many of whom were there for the first time and would not have been there at all except for the privilege of seeing the distinguished visitor—stood in the rain, some even without raincoats or umbrellas.

I heard one of the senators expressing regrets that we couldn't have had good weather, that it was a shame he would not get to see the fine views. It was a pleasant surprise to hear the president say, after having leaned out to see a few openings in the heavy rain clouds, "Well, it looks to me as though the rain may stop soon, in which case it will be much better than if it had not rained—we can then get the privilege of looking down on clouds below us, and across the clouds to the surrounding mountains." Within twenty or thirty minutes that is exactly what happened, and it was really a thrilling sight that greeted Mr. Roosevelt.

It was my privilege to present to him that day a special album of Great Smokies views that had been prepared by the Great Smoky Mountains Conservation Association for the occasion.

The president's next and only other visit to the Great Smokies was on Labor Day, 1940, at which time he dedicated the Great Smoky Mountains National Park at Newfound Gap. The dedication was more than six years after the official establishment of the park, on June 15, 1934.

Mrs. Roosevelt's only Great Smokies visit was in April of 1937, when she and her personal secretary spent several days during which she made a number of exploring trips from her Gatlinburg base. A park ranger escorted her on those trips to various sections of the park. I wanted to get some pictures of her and asked Superintendent J. Ross Eakin for permission to do so. Although he was opposed to the idea, he reluctantly gave permission for me to make pictures of the First Lady on the day that she was to visit Cades Cove. My pictures were to be made at the "apple stand" on the old road between Gatlinburg and Fightin' Creek Gap and nowhere else, and he so instructed Harold Edwards, the ranger who was her escort for the day. Knowing Mr. Eakin as I did, I knew better than to argue for permission to make pictures at a second stop.

The First Lady, Eleanor Roosevelt, during her only visit to the Great Smokies. She posed for me here, sitting on a rock, with the rushing water of the Sinks in the background, April 1937.

The First Lady cooperated wholeheartedly in the picture making at the announced picture spot, posing readily wherever I requested. While making those pictures, I took advantage of the opportunity to tell her about the treat that was in store for her in Little River Gorge, and especially at the Sinks. When I saw that she was planning to stop at the Sinks, I told her that I would like to have the privilege of getting some more pictures of her at that Little River Gorge spot. She replied that she would be glad to pose for me there, after which I suggested that *she* tell Mr. Edwards that more pictures were to be made at the Sinks. I knew full well that Harold would have refused if I had been the one to make the request, but I also felt sure that he would follow her instructions, even though they were contrary to the superintendent's orders. She did tell Mr. Edwards that more pictures were to be made at the Sinks, and he gladly complied.

She posed on the bridge, with the Sinks in the background. She then followed my suggestion that we go over to the bluffs on the other side of the river, where she posed two or three times more. I pointed out a spot about five feet from the edge of the bluff and asked if she would feel uneasy in posing there. She misunderstood just where I had indicated, and instead of stopping at the point that I had in mind she went on to the very brink of the bluff, where she posed without any indication of fear.

As had been the case with the president at the Shenandoah dedication, one might have gotten the impression that Mrs. Roosevelt's main purpose for being in Little River Gorge was to pose for my pictures.

HIKING NECESSITIES

Clothing and Equipment

One of the first things that need be done when a person becomes interested in hiking is to select and buy suitable equipment and clothing. In many cases there is a tendency to overdo it. It is almost as bad to have too much equipment as to have too little, because every needless item adds weight that has to be carried.

Having done extensive hiking for more than forty years, I am asked quite frequently, especially by mothers of youngsters who are planning to do some hiking, just what they should wear and what other things they should carry. Before giving the requested information, I usually warn that by far the most important thing for enjoyable hiking is the proper mental attitude. I always stress the fact that, regardless of what equipment or clothing they have, there is a strong probability that the new hiker will become painfully tired, cold, or wet—or, perhaps, thirsty—and unless they can experience physical discomfort without griping, it might be better not even to start. I then remind them that the results of the expected hardships are temporary, but that the rewards will linger long after any pain is forgotten.

If there is still an interest after such a warning I proceed to give a list of needed items, more or less in order of importance. My own experience leads me to the opinion that comfortable shoes should be at the top of the list. And, I further warn, for shoes or boots to be comfortable for mountain hiking they *must* be a little longer than one would select for city wear. This is true because half of the hiking will, of course, be down hill. With footwear that fits perfectly for level walking, the hiker will find, shortly after starting down the trail, that his or her toes are jabbing into the ends of the shoes with every step. Two or three miles of this will produce very sore toes, and perhaps some blisters.

I recall the time when Mrs. Campbell and I made the hiking club trip to Mt. Sterling. The ascent was made from Mt. Sterling Gap, which is only two and a half miles. But the return route down was by a seven-mile trail to Big Creek. Before we were halfway down, Mrs. Campbell's toes were so sore that something had to be done. She tried to make it barefooted, but her feet were too tender for that. I even considered the possibility of trying to carry her down the remaining four miles, but we both abandoned that as wishful thinking on my part. I then told her that only two alternatives seemed to be left. One was to cut out the toe of each shoe, and the other was to pitch her off the trail. We didn't like the second alternative, so I removed the toes of her shoes and she was then able to make it on her own power. The shoes had been selected carefully, she thought, but without realizing what would happen when her toes rubbed against the end of the shoes with every step. Thus, we learned the hard way that hiking shoes should—must is a better word—be a bit longer than what is needed for street wear.

Herbert Webster recalled another incident, which I had witnessed but forgotten, in which the lack of comfortable footwear almost ruined an otherwise enjoyable hike. Veteran hiker Walter Berry was wearing a new pair of shoes and had gone only a few miles when he learned that they were too tight for mountain use. After limping along for quite a while, he realized that he could not go on unless he got relief. This he did by cutting a hole in the side of the shoes. That helped for a short time, but other complications arose when his little toe jutted out through the newly made hole. Even this was all right for a short time, but when the group entered a section that was overgrown by saw briers, the toe very soon began to hang up on the briers. That was too much for Walter, and he removed the shoe and placed the foot on a nearby log, with the request that Guy Frizzell use Walter's ax to cut off the troublesome toe!

With these lessons clearly in mind, I made good use of them when I placed my order for a rather expensive pair of specially made boots. When the measurements were being made I told the clerk to specify that an additional half inch was to be added to the length. With that extra length, those boots were as comfortable the first time I wore them as they were by the time the tops had outlasted four pairs of soles.

On one occasion a relatively new member of the hiking club brought a visitor who had never done any hiking. As one of the designated leaders for that hike, which was an overnight affair, I noticed that the visitor was wearing lightweight pumps with medium-high heels. I asked if she had her hiking shoes in her pack, and was told that the only shoes she had brought were those she was wearing. She doubtless thought I was assuming too much authority when I told her that she would not be allowed to go with us without suitable footwear. I explained, however, that she would not be physically able to complete the trip with these shoes, even if she tried, and that it would be a miserable experience for her. It was further explained that she

My "specially made" boots (worn since May 1926) after twenty-five hundred miles of hiking in the Great Smokies. They have their fifth pair of soles—but the original laces—as seen here on September 30, 1935.

would also ruin the trip for at least one other person—the one who would have to assume the responsibility of getting her back to the car.

Yes, properly fitted shoes are absolutely essential for enjoyable hiking. They must be long enough and not too tight or too loose. Make no mistake about it, comfortable shoes are by far more important than all other items of clothing!

There must be some sort of hiking pack, of course, but the size and type should be determined by the kind of hikes that are to be made. For short one-day hikes, a very small pack will suffice, but for trips of several days, a larger one becomes a necessity. Many hikers prefer the Norwegian type of pack.

Next in importance, perhaps, is adequate rain gear. The absolute essentials in this category are a good poncho or raincoat and a rain hat. A poncho is preferable, especially if much hiking is to be done, because it not merely does a pretty good job of keeping the hiker dry, but also keeps his pack and sleeping gear dry. Many veteran hikers also use rain pants, and a few use rain shoes as well. Without the rain pants one's legs will get wet when it rains, but they soon dry out.

Rainwear that is suitable for summer use is not necessarily good for cold weather. Certain plastic items are quite good for summer because they are both efficient for protection and they have the added advantage of being lightweight. The late Dr. H. M. Jennison, former University of Tennessee botanist and hiking club president, was proud of such a raincoat—until he wore it on a cold winter hike to White Rock (later named Mt. Cammerer). As the stiff, cold winds hit that plastic coat, which had become as brittle as thin glass, it broke into splinters and in a matter of minutes all he had left was a few remnants which he brought back as souvenirs of the trip. A good woolen sweater or warm jacket is quite useful for wear at rest stops and while making camp. A change of other clothing is needed, especially for the longer hikes.

Experience has taught me that one does not always get back as soon as had been expected or planned. Because of this, it is tremendously important to carry a dependable source of light at all times, even on what may have been planned as rather short trips. Some hikers still prefer the old faithful candle lanterns—a folding metal frame with transparent windows on three sides, and with a holder for a medium sized candle in the bottom. This does not produce a very bright light, but all that is usually needed, and only one such lantern will serve for every two or three hikers. A few hikers like the old miner's carbide lamp. When that form of light is used it is important to carry an extra supply of carbide. Most hikers, perhaps, prefer to use flashlights. This is particularly true of beginners. It is a very efficient source of light, but when used there must be, for safety's sake, a good supply of batteries and an extra bulb or two.

Even when the trail is to follow or cross a stream, it is a good idea to carry a canteen of water. And if the route is to follow the main crest or any other high ridge for any considerable distance, the supply of water becomes something of a necessity.

If an overnight trip is involved, that, of course, calls for camping equipment. Even when it is expected that a Park Service trail shelter is to be used, it is a good idea to have a sleeping bag and rain gear. As many hikers have learned, those trail shelters are available on the first come, first served, basis, and it is not unusual to find the shelter completely filled when you arrive.

Other important equipment, especially for overnight trips, includes a good, stout—but lightweight—ax. If cooking is required, there must be the essential pots and pans. And, oh, my! How those things do weigh!

It is appropriate to emphasize further the importance of having a frame of mind that will permit the hiker to enjoy a trip in spite of temporary discomfort. As already stated, it is the best piece of "equipment" that a person can take on a hike. I witnessed a most impressive demonstration of that attitude many years ago at Charlies Bunion during a cold summer rain. The late Ernest Burtt, then a chalk-plate cartoonist for the *Knoxville Journal,* had told me that he wanted to make a hike into the Smokies with me. Ernest in those days made daily walks of from five to ten miles round-trip into the countryside around Knoxville; it was during these afternoon walks that most of his cartoon ideas were brought into focus. Before starting on the walk he would read the newspapers, then when he returned to his desk he usually had his cartoon for the next morning clearly outlined in his mind.

The Great Smokies hike that I planned for Ernest was from Newfound Gap to Charlies Bunion, a round-trip hike of eight miles. I had forgotten to tell him to bring some kind of rain gear, and he came without it. Jim Thompson also made the hike with us. Both Jim and I had our ponchos, as we always did, but Ernest was carrying only a lightweight coat.

While enjoying the thrilling view of Mt. LeConte and other peaks as we looked into the rugged Tennessee side of the jagged "Bunion," one of those sudden summer rains hit us, and Ernest was completely drenched within a very few minutes. Although it was mid-summer, the rain was very cold. Even Jim and I were getting a bit chilled, although we were still dry above our hips. Not so with Ernest. His teeth were chattering so loudly that we could have heard them from a considerable distance. He must have felt miserably cold, but to have heard his remarks one would not have known it.

Through all of his shivering he kept talking about what a wonderful privilege it was to have such an experience—first to view the sea of mountains spreading out before his eyes, then to see them quickly enveloped in a dense blanket of clouds. He didn't have to wait until he recovered from the chilling rain to know that he was being richly rewarded for his efforts. I'll have to admit that I learned a valuable lesson from him at that time.

Beginning hikers sometimes undertake a trip for which they are not prepared—especially not prepared psychologically. They find that the hike is so different from what they had expected that they become panicky or hysterical. Three such cases come to mind.

A woman who had done very little previous hiking made the mistake of accompanying the hiking club on a scheduled trip through Porters Flats to the state line, with the last half mile or less going up the bare face of Charlies Bunion. It was a cold winter day, with a little snow on the ground. It is important to know that practically all of the vegetation had been killed in one of the extensive forest fires in 1925, and that the 1927 cloudburst had swept away all of the remaining plants, even all of the humus, and left it deposited in huge logjams at the foot of the mountain.

When they reached the base of Charlies Bunion they became climbers rather than hikers. Occasionally jutting rocks were the only objects upon which to pull, or upon which to step while resting. Unfortunately, some of these rocks were not stable and went tumbling down the mountainside when a hiker pulled or stepped upon them. It is a miracle that no one was struck by one of those falling stones.

This unnamed woman finally made it safely up to the Appalachian Trail, near the crest of the mountain. At that point she became so hysterical that she almost had to be carried the remaining four miles, over a good trail, to Newfound Gap. It was not a matter of strength; she had plenty of that. It was that she had really gone through quite an ordeal during that dangerous climb, and she did not reach the breaking point until just after reaching safety.

Tom Duncan reports another case of a somewhat similar nature, except that it involved intense cold rather than actual danger. Tom Duncan, Ernest Fryar, Tom DeWine, another woman who will not be identified, and a few others were making a fairly long hike when the thermometer was down almost to zero. The woman, not adequately clothed for such a trip, became miserably cold and complained quite a bit about it. While hiking along the edge of a cliff, she was suffering so much that she threatened to jump off the precipice. Ernest and Tom Duncan pleaded with her to keep up her courage, saying that they would soon be back where she could again get warm, but they were making no progress whatever because she continued her threat.

Tom DeWine decided to try a different approach. He reprimanded the other men and said, "Let her go ahead and jump if that is what she wants to do!" That grim suggestion brought her to the realization that she wasn't in such a critical situation after all, and she went on without further complaint.

The third case of not being mentally or psychologically prepared for facing a strange situation occurred when Ted Sizemore, a fine physical specimen who then held the Southern YMCA heavyweight wrestling championship, was hiking with us through Huggins Hell. No member of the group had previously explored that rugged section of the park, but we had hiked through similar areas before. Ted, getting a bit tired anyway, began to worry about how much more of that kind of traveling we would have to do. As was reported earlier, he soon became panicky, almost hysterical, and even agreed to let Dutch Roth, a much smaller man, carry his (Ted's) pack along with his own pack.

Make due preparations for your hike, if possible. But please remember that you might become painfully tired, uncomfortably cold, and extremely thirsty—but that those conditions are very temporary and that there will be pleasant memories that will linger with you for many, many years.

FOOD

Many long hikes have been made in the Great Smokies. It is doubtful, however, if any other trip had so much advance planning and preparation as did the one made in 1941 by Mr. and Mrs. A. B. Crandall—Al and Alice—of Akron, Ohio. On this hike they spent ten consecutive days along the main crest from Deals Gap to Davenport Gap, a distance of seventy-two miles.

Although it was a definitely pleasant and enjoyable hike, it is likely that they received just as much pleasure throughout the preceding winter as they worked out, in minute detail, the plans for the upcoming hike. It is possible that they were not able to decide whether anticipation is, or is not, greater than realization. At least they will agree that their anticipation prolonged their period of enjoyment. This, however, was not their first hiking trip in the Smokies. I had been with them on Mt. LeConte, Chimney Tops, Gregory Bald and other points during their previous visits.

The decision to spend ten consecutive days along the main crest of the Smokies was made soon after their 1940 visit. Months ahead of the time for their departure they started working out the details—minute details of the forthcoming big venture. They knew, of course, that they could have hiked the seventy-two miles from Deals Gap to Davenport Gap in five days, but that was not the main point. Their real objective was to spend ten days in the high Smokies, allowing plenty of time for side trip exploring, picture making and just drinking in the charm and beauty of their surroundings.

As they started planning their menus, the first decision was that they would have to rely largely on dehydrated foods. What utensils, then, would they need, remembering that the overall weight must be limited as much as possible? Also, what clothing and bedding must they carry to prevent getting too cold at night, and to keep them as dry as possible, both day and night?

After weeks of enjoyable anticipation and planning, items in their list included two pack frames, two sleeping bags lined with down, and a woolen half envelope, with a total weight of 10.5 pounds; 8 pounds of photographic equipment; two sets of rain togs—ponchos, rain hats, steppers, and rubbers—for another 8.2 pounds of weight. Extra clothing weighed 8 pounds. Cooking and lighting equipment—an ax, cook kit, carbide headlamp, and a supply of carbide, firebrands and water bucket—added 7.9 pounds. Miscellaneous items—sewing kit, towels, candles, first-aid kit, soap, maps, and binoculars bore down a total of 12 pounds, thus bringing the total weight to 88.5 pounds before they got around to the all-important item of food. In their meticulous planning, they did not merely list the weight of the separate items, but computed the percentage of total weight that was represented by each item. The distribution of this part of their load placed 30 pounds in the pack that Alice was to carry, and left 58.5 pounds for Al.

Much of the time spent on the selection of foods was devoted, of course, to deciding what items of food they could include. Believe it or not, they wound up with 29 separate items of food. These were listed in the first of eight vertical columns on the page devoted to the various details of their food supply. Column number two told the form in which item was to be taken. The third column gave the amount of each item. The fourth gave the number of servings for each item of food. The fifth column showed the type of container in which the foods were packed. Column number six showed the container weights, without the food; column seven then gave the weights of the food in each container, while the ninth and last column gave the combined weights of containers and foods.

The total weight of foods and containers was 24.98 pounds. This, with the 88.5 pounds of other essentials, made up a total weight of 113.48 pounds. In a summary they mentioned the fact that each person was to consume a little less than a pound of dehydrated food per day—0.96 pounds, to be exact. As is shown in the accompanying copy of their food list, they were exact to a very fine degree.

Reference has already been made to the comparative values of anticipation and the realization. Many parents have suspected that their children's anticipation of Christmas often excels the thrills of opening packages and playing with toys or other gifts, because the anticipation is spread over a much longer period of time. I know full well what a thrill the Crandalls got from those ten days on the roof of Ole Smoky because some fifteen years earlier I made the same trip, in reverse direction—but using only nine days for it. But it calls for no stretch of imagination to realize that Al and Alice Crandall probably got as much, if not more, overall enjoyment from those months of planning and preparation.

While standing with them and other friends in the lobby of a Gatlinburg hotel a few days after they had completed that grand experience, we heard some man severely criticizing the National Park Service for having built the scenic park road across the Smokies. In reply, I expressed the opinion that the road, then new, would prove a big stimulus to hiking—that visitors would come as motorists, with no intention of ever doing any hiking. "But," I added, "some of these motorists will become fascinated with a trail that leads from the roadside into the dense forests and they will walk short distances along one or more of these trails." I further predicted that substantial numbers of motorists would, then, become hikers.

"That is exactly what happened to us," Al Crandall told the assembled group. "It was a surprise to us when we found that the trail appealed to us, but we were not properly dressed for hiking. On our next trip we brought a supply of hiking clothes, and in a few years we were thinking of ourselves as seasoned hikers. Without the roads inside the park we would have remained mere motorists for a long time, and thus would have missed the great joy of such trips as we have just completed."

As already implied, their ten-day hike was a grand experience in every respect. Food consumption was almost exactly as had been planned. Although they had carefully planned the mileage that should be covered each day, the time element left plenty of room for changes when needed or desired. When they reached a place of special charm or interest, they would linger to get the maximum enjoyment. Once they spent two nights at the same trail shelter, thus receiving some needed rest, but even more important was the joy of having more time at a favorite campsite.

The Crandalls returned for several later hiking-camping vacations in the Smokies. On those later trips, however, they had to be more alert for bears and dared not leave their campsites unattended. Bears by that time were becoming more numerous in the backcountry as well as along the park roads.

Although they lived several hundred miles from their favorite vacation spot, the Great Smokies, they learned to know these rugged mountains far better than most of the other visitors. In fact, there are relatively few people in the East Tennessee or western North Carolina areas who know as much about this park, or who derived as much pleasure from it, as did the Crandalls.

For long hikes in the mountains it becomes necessary to limit the weight of the packs as much as possible. One of the best ways in which this can be done is to use lightweight tents and other camping equipment. Another is to use dehydrated foods.

Provision Schedule
Mr. and Mrs. A. B. Crandall (Akron, Ohio)
Ten-Day Trip for Two Persons—56 Meals

Deals Gap to Davenport Gap (9-29 through 10-9, 1941)

Item	Form	Amount	Servings	Type of Container	Container Wt (lbs)	Food Wt (lbs)	Total Wt (lbs)
Eggs	Dried[1]	2 pts pk	12	Cans[6]	0.30[2]	1.10	1.40
Milk	Dried	2 quarts	50	Friction Can	0.70	2.34	3.04
Bread	Std	2 loaves	32	Original Pkg	0.13	2.00	2.13
Oat/Quik	Std	2 cups	8	Food Bag[3]	0.05	0.39	0.44
Wheatena	Std	1 1/3 cup	4	Food Bag	0.05	0.54	0.59
Beef	Canned	2 12-oz cans	4	Original Can	0.38	1.50	1.88
Tuna	Canned	2 7-oz cans	2	Original Can	0.32	0.88	1.20
Beef	Dried	1 2-oz can	1	Cellophane	0.09	0.13	0.22
Vegetables	Dried	5 oz	18	Food Bag	0.05	0.29	0.35
Spinach	Dried	2 oz	9	Food Bag	0.05	0.14	0.19
Butter	Std	2 lbs		Original Pkg	0.12	2.00	2.12
Cheese	Std[4]	1 lb		Metal Bag	0.06	1.00	1.06
Pancake Flour	Std	1/2 lb	2	Food Bag	0.05	0.50	0.55
Flour	Std	2 oz		Food Bag	0.05	0.13	0.18
Gravy	Dried	6 boxes	6	Original Pkg	0.06	0.41	0.47
Potatoes	Dried	3 pkgs	24	Original Pkg	0.03	0.83	0.86
Prunes	Dried	64 pieces	16	Food Bag	0.05	1.29	1.34
Apricots	Dried	66 pieces	10	Food Bag	0.05	0.98	1.03
Tea	Tablets	100 tblts	33	Tin Box	0.08	0.12	0.20
Coffee	Std	13.5 oz	18	9 Cloth Bags[5]	0.03	0.85	0.88
Sugar/Brn	Std	1.5 cups		Coffee Sack	0.03	1.10	1.13
Sugar/Wt	Std	3/8 cup		Coffee Sack	0.03	0.75	0.78
Soup	Cubes	54 cubes	40	Original Pkg	0.09	0.54	0.63
Salt	Std	1/3 cup		Can	0.06	0.23	0.29
Salt-Pep	Std	shaker		Tight Shaker	0.30	0.05	0.35
Cinnamon	Std	shaker		Tight Shaker	0.06	0.07	0.13
Candy	Std	1 lb		Can	0.15	1.00	1.15
Gum	Std	4 packs		Original Pkg	0.05	0.17	0.22
Vitamin	Std			Can	0.06	0.10	0.16
Total					3.53	21.43	24.96
% by wt.					14%	86%	100%

[1]Dehydrated; [2]Ounces expressed as decimals of pounds; [3]Standard cotton bags, paraffined; [4]Partially dried; [5]In thin cotton bags ready for pot, these carried in coffee sack; [6]Aluminum cans

Pounds Food Carried for Two Persons for 10 Days	21.43
Pounds Food Carried by Two Persons in 10 Days	19.07
Pounds Food Carried Per Person Per Day	1.07
Pounds Food Consumed Per Person Per Day	0.96

Personally, for hikes of only two or three days or less I much prefer to omit all dehydrated foods. I even use small cans of juices, meats and such. It is true that my pack, at the start of a trip, weighs a few pounds more than those of companions who are using dehydrated foods. But they, on the other hand, have to carry a lot of bulky pots and pans for which I have no need—and they have to carry them all the way.

While hiking the Appalachian Trail along the eastern half of the Smokies with a small group of friends from Baltimore, we were preparing supper and pitching our tents at the end of the second day. Because there were signs of possible rain, we set up our tents before giving any attention to food. While the friends were soaking their dehydrated foods, I completed my simple supper and was ready to retire before a sudden downpour of rain descended upon us. The others had eaten only their soup, while the remaining foods were still soaking.

Because the rain was such a hard and long one, the soup course was all they had to eat that night. That experience made me all the more willing to carry a few pounds more for the first day or so, in exchange for the greater convenience of preparing and eating my food. So, no dehydrated foods for me!

Hikers and mountain campers seem to have unlimited imagination when it comes to the selection of foods, especially foods to be prepared at a campfire.

One young hiker, who for obvious reasons shall remain unnamed, came up with so many unorthodox combinations of food that he soon became known as "Nastiness," except that it was always pronounced as "Nastness." To say that his culinary concoctions were something less than appetizing is quite an understatement!

I recall another occasion when Brockway Crouch, who had long been a bit partial to Silers Bald as a hiking destination, was chosen as one of the leaders of a hiking club overnight hike to Silers. That was long before Clingmans Dome Road was built, and the hike started at Fish Camp, which was a few miles upstream from Elkmont.

As soon as the tents were in place, we began to prepare food for the evening meal. A few fastidious campers had brought steaks, which they broiled over the campfire. I and a few others who made the practice of eating primarily for nourishment when camping opened our one can each of some favorite food—some using corned beef hash, some spaghetti and meat balls, and some other simple foods. Brockway, however, used a menu that was all his own, except that he was to share it with his big German Shepherd dog that, through the use of specially made "saddle-bags," had helped to carry Brock's load up the mountain.

He had brought a medium-sized stew pan into which he dumped a can of this and a can of that; winding up with a general mixture of four or five separate food items. When this mixture was well cooked, he emptied about half of it in his own platter, placed the remainder on a clean paper for the dog, and set the dog's portion aside out of reach until it cooled.

After a lapse of several minutes, he called the dog and placed the paper of food on the ground for the faithful companion and pack-carrier. Much to Brock's consternation, but to the amusement of the other campers, the dog sniffed at the food, then, with his right front paw, he began to pull loose soil and dirt over it until the food was completely covered.

For several years Brockway was not permitted to forget that incident.

℘   ℘   ℘

The ramp, a member of the lily family, is also known as wild leek in some parts of the country. To botanists it is *Allium tricoccum*. Although the taste is very similar to that of a sweet onion, the odor is much more pungent and longer lasting. Someone has said, "it is the sweetest tasting and foulest smelling plant that grows."

On one occasion, Mrs. Campbell, Mrs. L. R. Hesler, and Mrs. H. M. Jennison decided to stay at the foot of the mountain while their husbands and others made a rainy day hike. As the wives were taking a short walk, they were caught by a hard rain and ran to a nearby home for shelter. The family—which will not be identified—and some guests were eating their Sunday dinner, an item of which must have been generous helpings of ramps. The odor was so strong that the wives decided they had better get on back to the cars, rain or no rain.

On another occasion several hikers camped near Tapoco, North Carolina, preparatory to a hike to Hangover, which is a high peak that is partly in Cherokee National Forest, on the Tennessee side of the state line, and partly in Nantahala National Forest, on the North Carolina side. A lad of about ten years was an interested spectator as the hikers prepared and ate their supper and as they pitched their tents. Finally he mustered nerve enough to ask if he could make the hike with them the next day. He was told to bring his own lunch and to be there early the next morning. When he arrived, it was easily evident that he had not brought any lunch. When it was mentioned to him he just shrugged his shoulders and said, "I'll just eat me a mess of ramps."

During the early park days Dr. H. M. Jennison, University of Tennessee professor of botany, served as a seasonal naturalist for the park. On a day off from work, he took his wife and a few friends—musician Frank Nelson, Jim Thompson, and me—to see the big holly tree, more than two feet in diameter, on Meigs Creek.

As we came down the Meigs Creek trail, below the big holly, we found a sizeable patch of ramps, and all of us ate some of those "sweet tasting and foul smelling" tubers. As we returned to Knoxville, several hours later, the other men stopped off at the Tennessee School for Deaf for a Rotary Club function, and I took Mrs. Jennison on to her home. As I escorted her toward the side door her daughter, Dorothy, opened the door and greeted us. But, while her mother was still six or eight feet away, we heard the daughter exclaim, "Mother! What in the world have you been eating?"

Ramps are highly regarded by mountain people. During the springtime they are eaten in great quantities—not just as a food but also as a tonic and health giver. Since most mountain people eat ramps, there seems to be no problem concerning the odor.

CAMPFIRES

Do you know how to build a campfire when the wood is wet?

If not, you are not likely to be able to get a camping permit from park rangers. And, what is much more important, you are likely to suffer serious consequences if you do attempt an overnight hike after a hard, long rain or after there has been a deep snow on the ground for a few days. All potential campers need to remember that it is necessary to obtain permits from park rangers before building a fire within the park boundaries.

By far the most urgently important factor in fire building is to have a completely dependable source of fire. The most widely used of these are wooden-stemmed matches—often called kitchen matches—dipped in paraffin, and/or carried in a waterproof container. Sporting goods stores carry such boxes. Another good source of fire, for those who use that source of light, is a carbide miner's lamp.

Experienced hikers and backcountry campers have learned that the best source of wood with which to get a fire started in wet weather is to select branches of a fallen tree that are sticking up vertically. Upright branches do not absorb as much water as do those that are horizontal. Branches up to three or four inches in diameter may be split into small splinters. Usually the center portion of such branches will be dry, or approximately so. Another good trick is to select the very small twigs, the size of an ordinary pencil or smaller, that are standing in an upright position.

Even with these precautions it is advisable to carry with you something that will ignite quickly and which will produce a sustained flame long enough to start a fire with your main fuel supply. Some campers prefer a few splinters of rich (resinous) pine. Others carry several short pieces of candle to be used in getting damp pieces of wood started burning. Still another fire-building aid that a few others and I used several years ago, but which apparently is no longer available, was a resinous briquette. It was made of sawdust, which had been impregnated with pine resin and pressed into oblong blocks about three inches long. A somewhat similar product, except for size, is still available from such sporting goods stores as Abercrombie and Fitch, of New York, and L. L. Bean, of Freeport, Maine. It comes in sizes about the same as dominos, and is described as "fire-kindlers." The advantage of this, and the former resinous briquette, is that they are easy to ignite, and they made a hot flame for several minutes—long enough to ignite damp or even wet wood.

Equally important, I have found, is a two-foot length of small rubber tubing—such as that used on a syringe. By placing one end of the tube near the beginning fire and blowing gently through the other end, you can actually get a fire started when all of the wood is at least damp. We long ago designated this bit of rubber tube as an "inspirator." Call it what you will, it can be a tremendously important bit of equipment for use on a camping trip.

Hikers who use the trail shelters along the crest of the Smokies and elsewhere find it increasingly difficult to get a supply of wood near the shelters. Considerate hikers make it a practice to leave at least a small amount of wood inside the shelter so the next group to camp there will have some dry wood with which to start their fire, and they do this even if the previous users have not been so thoughtful.

Joel H. Anderson, Jr., a hiking friend of many years standing, reported having seen a pathetic effort at fire building on the part of a group of teenage boys and an adult leader. At Ice Water Spring, on the Appalachian Trail about three miles east from Newfound Gap, Joel watched them trying to start a fire, with wet wood, by using large quantities of toilet tissues and quantities of gasoline. Obviously, any man who is so ignorant about fire building should never dare take boys on an overnight trip, even in the summer.

Herbert M. Webster reported an interesting campfire experience—at least it is interesting in retrospect—in which he and a young companion lost their way coming down the south slope of Mt. LeConte and then he lost his shirt.

His companion was Donald Wilburn, a fourteen-year-old Boy Scout, who was an experienced hiker—and who later failed to return from a flying mission during World War II. They climbed LeConte by the old Rainbow Falls path. Using only a box camera, Herbert made an exceptionally good picture of the falls, which he said is the best picture of the falls that he ever made.

Incidentally, at one of their rest stops they were overtaken by Jack Huff, who was building the lodge on Mt. LeConte. As Jack went on by them, setting a rather fast pace with his exceptionally long stride, Herbert noticed that Jack's huge pack was loaded with just one item of food, loaves of bread, and in his hand he was carrying a big iron wedge that he was to use in splitting logs for building his new lodge.

Herbert and Donald slept on the ground that night near the lodge. He said that neither of them had ever seen, much less used, a sleeping bag. After making the usual trips, to Myrtle Point and Cliff Top, they started down the mountain with the intention of following the old Bear Pen Hollow trail, then not even a clearly beaten path. Within ten minutes they realized that they were not on the trail, so they decided to find their way over to a stream and to follow it down to the Newfound Gap highway.

"This might have been the proper decision," Herbert recalls, "but it resulted in the roughest experience I ever had in the mountains. Unless you have tried to make your way through tangled growths while carrying heavily loaded packs you would have no conception of the ordeal of penetrating the lower part of Huggins Hell," he added. "At times we became so entrapped in the laurel and saw briers that we had to assist each other in getting out of some of those traps. At times we could make more progress on top of the shrubs than could be made through or under them. Part of the time we could make better progress in the stream, so we alternated between rock hopping and fighting the dense tangles of shrubs."

Herbert recalls that bad matters were made worse when he noticed that darkness was about to overtake them. Hoping to get out of such a rough and unfamiliar area while there was still some light, he now admits that he panicked and started running down the streambed, jumping from rock to rock. It was a bit embarrassing, he said, to be reminded by his young companion that such speed was likely to cause an accident, so he slowed down to a safer pace.

The situation improved very quickly, however, when they unexpectedly came out into an opening that they later learned was Grassy Patch—now Alum Cave Parking Area—just before dark. They were soaked to the skin and were becoming uncomfortably cold. They gathered enough wood to get a good fire going. Realizing that they would need lots of fuel if they were to keep the fire going all night, as they hoped to do, they even pulled long poles out of the creek and piled them on the fire to dry out so they would burn. Wet clothing was hung on the ends of the poles to dry while they searched for more wood.

"When returning to the campfire with a new load I detected an odor that was quite different from the pleasant smell of wood smoke," he said. "Making a dash for the fire I was horrified when I saw that my shirt had been left too close to the fire and that all of it except the collar and one sleeve had gone up in smoke."

Herbert said that the loss of the shirt—the only one he had brought—caused no particular discomfort. But it did cause some embarrassment and required a lot of explanations as he rode the bus from Gatlinburg back to Knoxville, and then on to his home by the Fountain City streetcar.

Most hikers, it seems, prefer to do their hiking in groups, some large and some small. There are, however, a few who prefer solo hiking.

In my more than forty years of hiking I made only one solo hike and that was by accident. I had waited for others who were late, while the remainder of a family group went ahead on their climb over and around the boulders on the old Rainbow Falls trail to Mt. LeConte. After waiting longer than I thought to be necessary, I set out by myself.

Before starting I decided to use this situation for a little test. Just how long did it take to climb LeConte without rushing, and without lingering too long at rest spots? My time on previous hikes ranged from three to seven hours, depending on how much amateur botanizing I was doing. As I had planned, my rest stops, except the one at the falls, were just long enough to note the time and pedometer reading and write them down on a notepad. I didn't even sit down. I had planned to rest for five minutes at the falls, but I found that two minutes was sufficient. With such a schedule the time was two hours and fifteen minutes. As a test, it was interesting—but I much prefer to share the many pleasures of hiking with at least one or two friends.

One of the worst things about solo hiking is the element of danger. There are many ways in which a hiker may have an accident—a sprained foot or leg; a fall, possibly with a broken bone; or one may even have a heart attack. In such an emergency there should be at least one other person so he could go for needed help. Better still, there should be at least three members of any party. In the admittedly unlikely event of an accident, one could stay with the injured person while the other went for help.

Three Great Smokies tragedies might have been due directly to unwise solo hiking, although it is just as possible that one or more of them belong in the category of suicide.

The first of these "solo hiking tragedies" in the Great Smokies came to light on April 23, 1938, when Jack Huff found the frozen body of Miss Sue Grace Ingraham, a Knoxville nurse, just off the trail near Cliff Top of Mt. LeConte. It is believed that the body had been there since November of 1937, a period of approximately five months.

Several days after Miss Ingraham's body was found, George Hines was making an announcement at the Knoxville High School chapel exercises in which he was urging a good turnout for a forthcoming hike of a school group. Prof. W. E. Evans, principal of the school, asked George what he would have done if he had been the one to find that frozen body.

"I would have made a new trail straight down the side of the mountain," George replied.

The next solo hiking tragedy occurred on January 30, 1941, when the body of Tute Bright—no address given—was found near the three-thousand-foot elevation marker on the North Carolina side of U.S. 441. The young man had been given supper at the Kephart Prong Civilian Conservation Corps camp and had walked up the highway while hoping to catch a ride across to the Tennessee side of the park.

The occurrence of the third tragedy—or suicide—was learned on Sunday, March 25, 1962, when ramp gatherers found a few of what was believed to be human bones at the foot of a cliff known by some in prepark days as "Fort Harry" and known by others as the "Brownlow Rock." It is a few hundred yards up the mountain from the Buckeye Nature Trail. Other bones were found later, but it was not until Chief Ranger Tom Ela and Ranger John Morrell found the skull that they were certain that it was human bones that had been found by the ramp hunters. Although there was very little information that could be classed as a clue to the victim's identity, the painstaking and detailed work of specialists in the FBI laboratory in Washington, D.C., in September identified the victim as being Louis Bronson LeDuc, Jr., of Camden, New Jersey. The identification was based largely on dental work that had been done. The Park Service report on this case indicated that Mr. LeDuc's death could have been caused by a snakebite, a fall from the nearby cliff, or from exposure following an accident in which a leg was broken.

News of the victim's identification was carried in Knoxville newspapers just a few days after five members of my family returned home from a trip that included several interesting hours spent in the FBI building in Washington. While there, we were shown how several mysteries had been solved, and criminals identified and caught, with extremely slim bits of information. After reading about the Great Smokies case that the FBI had just solved, we realized that Mr. LeDuc's identification might have been made while we were in the FBI Building.

☞   ☞   ☞

Many hikers have reached the crest of the Smokies at points a few miles from the intended destination because of having made the wrong turn at the forks of a creek or at a trail junction. Only once, however, have I found myself back at the starting point after hiking for several miles on what I, and other members of the group, thought to be the correct trail. That is a very humiliating and frustrating experience.

On a scheduled club hike our group started from near Smokemont and headed up toward Hughes Ridge. We were to cross that ridge and hike down to Raven Fork, which we were to follow upstream to Three Forks, at the lower edge of the wilderness area just across the mountain from the Greenbrier wilderness area. As we reached the crest of Hughes Ridge, we found an unexpected trail junction. After some discussion we decided that we should take the fork to our left, and did so. A few of the hikers feared that we were not headed in the right direction, but no one was prepared for what we saw a little later. Just try to imagine our disgust when we realized that we had made a circuitous trip back to the starting point we had left just two hours earlier!

It was too late to start again that night, so we made camp and fought swarms of black gnats most of the night. With all the extra mileage to cover on the two remaining days of a three-day hike, we made an early start the next morning, and made it a point of special interest to take the correct turn at the top of Hughes Ridge.

Herbert Webster recalls that hiker Tom Brightwell had brought his brother, Walter Brightwell, along. Before we had gone very far, Walter complained that there was something in his shoe, but he kept up with the faster pace and only occasionally did he make further reference to his discomfort. When he did complain again, he still refused to take time out to remove the gravel, or whatever it might be that was bothering him. When we finally reached Three Forks, he pulled off his shoe and socks and found that the offender was a nail in his shoe, and that it had made a hole as big as a match head in the bottom of his foot!

There was still time for some good swimming in the deep pool where the three smaller streams come together. And there was a lot of conversation. Charlie Gibson told about a previous trip he had made, saying that he had, on the earlier trip, spent the night in the crude cabin that was still standing at the time of our trip. Charlie had insisted that the cabin door be left open, but finally responded to the insistence of companions that the door be closed. As he reached out to place his hand on the edge of the door so he could close it he declared that some animal, probably a bear, had licked his hand before he could get the door closed.

Because of that bear story, Mrs. Campbell and a few other wives in the group got less sleep that night than would have been expected after a good long hike.

✐   ✐   ✐

Having been hiking companions on many backbreaking trips in the Smokies, Herbert Webster and Boyd Potter spent an afternoon in Greenbrier Cove hunting for a huge chestnut tree and a big poplar tree that they had seen some ten years earlier. They camped near the hiking club cabin. Early the next morning they were awakened by a rain that plagued them the remainder of the day. Although they resumed their search for the big trees for which the Porters Flats section of Greenbrier is famous, they could not find the same ones.

It was 4:00 P.M. when they decided to start back to Gatlinburg by way of Trillium Gap. It was still raining hard as they reached and crossed the several streams between Trillium Gap and Gatlinburg, with the result that those normally small branches and creeks were then so swollen that it was difficult to cross them. In the meantime it was getting dark, and they had to rely on their flashlight in making the crossings. It became difficult to find the trail after crossing a stream.

"Although my boots were already wet, I was reluctant to wade a swollen stream with them on," Herbert told me, "so I decided to carry my boots as I walked barefooted across the creek, which by that time was a raging torrent. After I had gone only a few feet into the deep water, I caught my feet in some debris and almost fell. Worse, however, I dropped one of the boots. In consternation I saw it carried away from me and swept toward a drop off that would have taken it into the semidarkness," he recalled.

He said that it would have been futile to try to overtake it by getting into the stream, so he decided to run along the bank in the hope that he could head it off. As he held to a small tree at the edge of the creek with one hand he saw that the floating boot had been slowed by some obstruction, and luckily he was able to retrieve it.

"Under other circumstances this situation would have been quite amusing, but such was not the case that night," Herbert said. "Naturally, I then put the wet boots back on my feet and took the water as I came to it."

One creek was so deep that they felt it would be too risky to attempt a crossing in the darkness, so they went back to where they had seen another trail leading off to the left and followed it. This led them to what they later learned was Baskins Creek, which they followed down to Gatlinburg. They reached their car about 11:00 P.M.

"Jack Huff's hospitality and a hot shower soon made us forget our weariness," Herbert said, "but the frequent recollection of a nearly lost boot made us realize more fully how important a simple piece of clothing or equipment can be on a mountain trip."

Alert hikers will find many things of interest along their trails or untrailed routes. Previously unknown species of trees, shrubs, and wildflowers may be discovered. Unfamiliar species of birds and animals will be encountered. Unique cliffs and other rock formations may be seen in many parts of the park. These things will provide rewards for those who take the time to look for them. It is not easy to identify them properly, but still greater enjoyment will come from checking out those plants, birds, or animals to ascertain what they really are.

Sometimes, though, we are a bit inclined to jump to conclusions or make erroneous identifications. In July of 1928, on the first hiking club trip along the tumbling waters of Roaring Fork Creek, from the spring at LeConte Lodge down toward Gatlinburg we found a high wall of solid rock rising almost one hundred feet perpendicularly above the edge of the stream. Approximately halfway up the sheer cliff there was a pyramidal hole in which we could see what was obviously the nest of some large bird.

Our somewhat vivid imaginations told us that it must be an eagle's nest. So, when we returned to Knoxville, we reported to Brockway Crouch that we had found an eagle's nest. By that time there was no question in our minds as to its identity. Not so with Brock, who was an active member of the local bird study club. He immediately considered an exploratory trip so he could see for himself what kind of nest it was.

A short time later Brock and W. W. Stanley, a University of Tennessee entomologist who was then better known to hiking companions as "Alkali Ike," made careful plans for the inspection trip. They realized that the only way by which they, or either of them, could actually reach the nest would be to anchor a long rope to a tree at the top of the cliff and climb down the rope, and that is what they attempted. Since they were using a small, strong rope it was decided to suspend a doubled portion, with a loop that would reach just below the bottom of the nest site. With this done, Brock climbed down and placed one foot in the loop. But there was a slight over-hang, which they hadn't noticed, and Brock could not reach the nest without swinging himself back and forth until he was able to place one hand on the ledge at the bottom of the nest.

Even before he actually touched the ledge he saw that the nest was that of a raven—not an eagle. This he was able to determine by the fact that the nesting material was much too small to be that used by an eagle. Just before Brock started to climb down the doubled rope, Ike went to the ground at the base of the cliff from which vantage point he had planned to make pictures of Brock's activities.

But before he made a single picture the unexpected happened. The part of the ledge to which Brock was holding pulled out, which threw him off balance. He fell head downward but managed to catch one foot in the loop of the rope, thus preventing an immediate fall of some fifty feet to the ground at the base of the cliff. Brock, who then weighed 200 pounds, was a bit stunned. Try as hard as he could, he could not pull himself up to where he could again get his hands on the rope so he might be able to climb back up to the top. Ike, who weighed only 145 pounds, realized that he could not come down the rope and carry Brock back up to safety. The situation became desperate; something had to be done, and soon.

It was agreed that Ike would start down one strand of the rope a short distance then grasp the other strand tightly and cut it just above where he was holding it. He was then to climb down slowly, thus lowering Brock as the loop was lowered. But that is not the way it worked out. When Ike cut the strand he was not able to hold it, and Brock dropped suddenly, landing on his head and shoulders. Ike then climbed on down the single remaining strand and joined his stunned companion.

Brock's life was saved by the fact that the ground where he fell was a very steep slope—at least as steep as an average house roof. So, when he landed, he was not stopped completely but rolled down the slope for several feet. Miraculously, there were no broken bones, but he was pretty badly bruised.

By this time there was not much daylight left, and there was no trail for the first two miles of the return trip. Incidentally, Roaring Fork flows through some exceptionally rough terrain, with a number of sizable water-falls, between the raven's nest and the Cherokee Orchard–Trillium Gap Trail.

Brock was able to walk but used Ike somewhat as a crutch. The progress was very slow because the dense tangles of rhododendron that lined the banks and the extreme steepness of the stream made it impossible to walk very far in the streambed, with the result that darkness soon descended on them. Ike, using a miner's carbide lamp for illumination, had to leave Brock frequently while he explored for the best route around the several waterfalls.

He told me recently that at one point he was unable to find his way back to Brock until he had wandered back and forth for about ten or fifteen min-utes. The way he did find him was by seeing the light from his lamp reflect-ed from the eyes of Brock's dog. He had refrained from calling to Brock because he didn't want to frighten him. (Brock admitted in March of 1967 that he had never until that time known that Ike was "lost.")

After working their way laboriously down to where Roaring Fork crossed the Cherokee Orchard–Trillium Gap Trail, the going was much faster. Even so, it was long past midnight when they reached the home of Sherman Clabo, who lived in the last house up Roaring Fork. And it was almost day-light when they reached Fort Sanders Hospital in Knoxville.

Examinations made there confirmed the belief that there were no bro-ken bones. Brock did complain some about a severe pain in his jaw. His dentist, after examining the patient, gave a quick jerk to Brock's head, the jaw snapped back in place, and all was well again.

After resting just one week in the hospital, Brock was back on the job at his retail flower store, a bit worse for the wear, but with the satisfaction that he had turned our eagle's nest into a raven's nest.

🍂   🍂   🍂

Most hikers, sooner or later, become deeply interested in observing and learning more about the wildflowers seen along the trails of the Great Smokies. Others, however, care little or nothing about the identities of the trees, shrubs, and other wildflowers.

There is one plant, however, that it would be well for all hikers to be able to identify so they can then be governed accordingly. It is the woods nettle (*Laportea canadensis*).

When our oldest son, Clinton, was about ten years old, he accompanied a visitor and me on a hike up the Road Prong trail, then along the crest of the mountain to Newfound Gap, and returning along the Newfound Gap Highway.

Clinton was wearing a pair of shorts, and this seemed to be appropriate clothing until we were pushing our way through the weeds that had overgrown much of the trail along the crest of the mountain. It took but very little of this until Clinton complained, "Dad, something is biting my legs."

At first I did not suspect what the real culprit was. But when he complained again, at which time he made the complaint a bit emphatic, I looked at his legs—which by that time were quite red and irritated all the way from the tops of his shoes to the bottom of his shorts.

Then I noticed that we were wading through a dense growth of woods nettle. With that discovery, I had no choice but to carry him until we had gotten completely away from the nettles.

Both the leaves and the stems of this plant are covered with tiny barbs that produce a stinging sensation very much like that of a bee sting. I suspect that Clinton suffered more pain from these stinging nettles than I later suffered from the bite of a rattlesnake.

NATURE

Reforestation

Hiking through a cut-over and burned-over area during the first stages of reforestation can not be classed as a delightful experience, especially at an elevation where the dominant plant to follow in the wake of the forest fire is the blackberry. Albert G. "Dutch" Roth and I have firsthand information on the subject.

A hiking club trip was scheduled to start at the junction of Twenty-Mile Creek and the Little Tennessee River, with the fire tower on Shuckstack, on the North Carolina side of the park, as the destination. That is an easy trip, even after a rather long drive to the starting point. Since Dutch and I felt the urge to do quite a bit more hiking, we left Knoxville a few hours earlier and started our hike at Deals Gap, where we followed the main crest up to Parsons Bald. That was familiar country for us. The route from Parsons Bald down, approximately along Twenty-Mile Creek, was to be new territory, and we had no idea just what to expect. For a short distance our main problem was to work our way through fairly thick growths of young black locust trees, with their numerous heavy thorns. We thought that was bad enough, but we were very soon in a situation somewhat like going from the proverbial frying pan into the fire. As we left the locust trees behind, we found increasingly dense growths of tall, thorny blackberries. At times we were able to find openings through which we could walk, but most of the way the briers were so big and growing so close together that we had to use strong sticks to make an opening through which we could pass.

Most of the route was along the abandoned grade of an old logging railroad. The only advantage we got from that fact, however, was that it did indicate the general route we had to follow. It seemed to us that the blackberries along the old roadbed were even more dense than elsewhere. Dutch and I had helped mark many miles of park trails, and we agreed that these blackberry plants were large enough for blazing, as in trail marking.

Our progress through that three or more miles of blackberries was so tortuously slow that we did not reach the point where Twenty-Mile Creek crossed the Deals Gap–Bryson City road until after most of the hikers, who were making only the regular trip, had already started up the short graded trail to the Shuckstack fire tower. We joined the late arrivals and accompanied them. To have the privilege of once again hiking on a graded trail, with no blackberries or locust stickers to snag us, was a pleasant contrast. This enabled us to quicken our pace a bit, and we reached the destination almost as soon as had been expected when we had started the "warm-up" part of our trip.

The Shuckstack tower, which is located on a sharp knob with slopes dropping off steeply in three directions, provided dramatic views of the deep gorge through which the Little Tennessee River flows. From the tower we could see that the forested slopes of the flanking mountains rose very steeply from the river's edge. A veritable sea of mountain ranges spread into a most pleasing panorama as far as one could see. It was, indeed, a fitting climax for the hike, even for the rather strenuous and somewhat painful part made by Dutch and me.

It is appropriate that we note a radical change in the landscape south and east from the Shuckstack tower that was made about 1945, following the 1944 completion of the very high Fontana Dam, which had been built by the Tennessee Valley Authority (TVA). Since that time the most conspicuous part of the view from Shuckstack tower has been the clear water of the lake that was formed by that dam. Much of the beauty of this lake is provided by the rugged and green-clad mountains that surround it. The relocated Appalachian Trail crosses Shuckstack en route to Fontana Dam.

It takes very little of the type of hiking that Dutch Roth and I encountered between Parsons Bald and the mouth of Twenty-Mile Creek to make one give thought to the extremely slow process of natural reforestation, following the devastation wrought by timber cutting and forest fires. Long before the first part of that hike had been completed, we found ourselves wishing that the process of reestablishing a forest could have been much more rapid.

The frequent rains of the Great Smokies would enable a lush ground cover to get started very quickly after an area had been burned, but since there were no mature trees left to supply seed for a new forest, a variety of "weeds" and blackberry plants provided the initial covering. For hikers, this is unfortunate—as Dutch and I learned from experience.

Most of the few tree seeds that do fall, or are carried, into the masses of blackberry plants are choked out by the dense shade soon after they germinate. A few, however, do live and eventually reach out above the blackberries, thus starting a new phase of the natural process of reforestation.

Foresters tell us that within a few decades there is a nearly solid stand of trees—usually yellow poplar (tulip), maple, and a mixture of short-life trees such as sassafras, sourwood, and fire cherry. These trees then choke out the blackberries, with the result that very few of them will remain as long as forty or fifty years. The foresters also report that in areas such as we traversed on this hike, the climax forest is not completely established until about seventy-five or one hundred years after the forest fire. This permanent forest, composed largely of oak, hickory, maple, and yellow poplar, then settles down for a few hundred years to the problem of increasing the size of the component trees before it again will resemble a virgin forest. The complete cycle of natural reforestation is, indeed, a very lengthy process!

⌀   ⌀   ⌀

As farmers in the foothills sections of the Great Smokies sold their land and moved out, their abandoned fields quickly started the slow but sure process of reverting to forests. The first new growth in many cases was blackberries, with various species of trees gradually reaching up above the blackberries. Fields near pine forests were soon covered by extremely dense stands of fast-growing young pine trees.

Many other evidences of previous habitation began to disappear. Many old homes, barns, and other structures were razed, and those not worth the cost of dismantling were burned—at times when there was no danger of starting forest fires, such as just after a general rain. Most of the old homes have long since disappeared, with a few selected exceptions being preserved as "museum pieces," such as in Cades Cove, Cataloochee, and a few lesser areas. Remaining indications of abandoned homesites are old apple trees, bright clusters of jonquils in early spring, a few rose bushes and such—all of which will also disappear in a few more decades.

Some of the most durable and picturesque remnants of an earlier civilization are the several widely scattered rock fences, many of which were still in perfect condition as late as 1967. These loosely laid rock walls made perfect fences, especially for the confinement—or exclusion—of hogs and cattle. There was, however, another function that they filled. Much of the mountain land was covered with loose rocks, head size and larger, as well as by trees. The rocks had to be removed before the fields and gardens could be cultivated. And, as erosion uncovered still more rocks, they, too, had to be removed for easier cultivation. The most logical thing to do with them, therefore, was to build the rock fences. Such fences needed very little repairing. Visitors who see these interesting rock "walls" can readily see what they are, but not necessarily why they were built.

Another, and perhaps even a longer-lasting reminder of an earlier civilization, is seen in a very few small streams, portions of which served for short distances as a wagon road. Steel-rimmed wagon wheels cut definite grooves into the solid rock stream beds during many years of use as wagon roads, especially where the stream was so narrow that the wheels necessarily followed within a few inches of the same place each trip up or down the creek. In the pioneer days road-grading equipment was nonexistent, with the result that at places where there was no level land beside the stream it was necessary to use the streambeds as roads.

As already indicated, streams that doubled as roads were rare. The only park stream in which I have seen the wheel-carved ruts is the one alongside the old Anderson Road a short distance north (upstream) from where this little creek flows into Laurel Creek. The stream bed is no longer used as a roadway because the Civilian Conservation Corps boys, with good equipment, did the necessary grading to keep the road on dry ground, whereas not only did the early settlers not have the equipment, they also had more urgent work to do.

This interesting but mute evidence of the primitive civilization is not likely to be seen unless it is pointed out by one who knows the story. Arthur Stupka, then chief naturalist for the Great Smokies, first brought it to my attention about 1936. The next and only other time that it was called to my attention was in March 1967, when horseman Al Lewis told me about it and showed it to me as he was conducting a special horseback trip for granddaughters Melissa "Missy" Campbell and Rebecca "Becky" Campbell and me.

Charles S. Dunn, former chief ranger for the Great Smokies, who now lives at his old boyhood home place beside the Anderson Road just outside the park, told me in 1967 that the stream in which we see the wagon-made ruts was originally known as the "Near Branch." Whereas the stream alongside the Anderson Road south of Laurel Creek—the one flowing from Bote Mountain—was at the same time known as the "Far Branch." Some people have thought or assumed that the wagon-wheel stream had borne the name of "Spence Deadening Branch." That stream, however, flows into "Near Branch" a short distance north of Laurel Creek.

It is quite likely that there are several other streams inside the park with solid rock bottoms that have been rutted by wagon wheels, but the only other one that I ever saw was near the headwaters of Tuckahoe Creek, in the Kodak section of Sevier County and some twenty-five miles from the Great Smokies. For a distance of almost a mile the road to my grandfather's home followed the rocky bed of Tuckahoe Creek.

A national park with no roads or trails would preserve the wilderness qualities of the area, but only an extremely small portion of the public could see and enjoy its great beauty. The congressional act that created the National Park Service gave that conservation agency the double responsibility of preserving the area and making it possible for the public to enjoy it. This, of course, necessitated the building of a few roads and a network of trails. The trails were to serve in helping to protect the area from fire or vandalism and to give the public easier access to points of major beauty and interest.

Such construction projects unavoidably create a large number of small temporary scars. Except for the fact that nature soon provides a new vegetation cover for those scars, much of the construction could not be justified. Visitors who derive so much enjoyment from the Great Smokies can find a number of good examples of how thoroughly, and at times how quickly, nature does heal the scars—sometimes providing even greater beauty in doing so.

The old Road Prong trail, starting near the base of Chimney Tops and extending up to Indian Gap, is a good example. Visitors always have high praise for the charm and beauty of this trail and of the immediate trailside. A great variety of plants thrive there, with the result that the visitor is hardly aware of the fact that this was an old wagon road built by Cherokee Indians as their contribution to the Confederate cause at the beginning of the Civil War. In building the road, there was no thought whatever for preserving the beauty. The banks were cut very steeply so the road could be opened quickly and with as little effort as possible. Yet, the steepness of the banks is not what the visitor now sees. They are completely and beautifully blanketed with shrubs and wildflowers. Trail-building methods now call for gently sloping banks, to encourage a quicker covering.

But one of the best examples of a speedy restoration is the wall of beautiful green foliage seen along the upper edge of Clingmans Dome Road, especially along the last mile or so of that road. When the engineers were selecting the route for the road, it was decided to place it at the upper edge of an area that was devastated by forest fires in 1925, shortly after timber cutting was completed. Trees that were still living on the slopes above the road had no low branches, since they had grown up alongside other trees that had been killed by the fire. This meant that the new road was bordered by a fire scald on the lower side and on the upper side by tall trees that resembled telephone poles with a few green branches near the top. They were, however, still alive—at least for a very few years. Grading for the road building caused the water table to be lowered to the point that the trees on a strip less than a hundred yards in width died of thirst.

In the meantime, large quantities of seeds from those doomed trees, and from other nearby trees that were not to be killed, had fallen on that narrow strip of ground near the top of the road bank. Even before the old trees had died, there was a dense ground cover of young spruce and fir. Being several feet above the road level, those beautiful young trees were not visible to passing visitors, and the result was a rather depressing sight for a short period of time. It was only a few years, however, until those thousands of young trees were tall enough to be seen and enjoyed from the road level.

Within three decades—a short time in the life of a forest—the whole picture had changed, and changed very much for the better. By that time visitors were seeing a solid wall of rich green foliage that reached all the way from the ground up to the tops of the old trees, thus shielding the portion of the old trees that had the appearance of telephone poles.

What we had above the road, just after the road was built, was something less than beautiful. That was followed, temporarily, by a "brown fringe of death," but shortly replaced, permanently, by a "green fringe of beauty." Such is the healing power of nature, especially in the Great Smokies, where the abundant rainfall and the rich soil combine to produce rapid growth.

As a result, we have a network of wonderful trails and a few miles of highly scenic park roads that make it possible for park visitors to get much more enjoyment from their trips. A few of the trails lead to beauty spots that had been unknown to hikers. Ramsey Cascades is an example. Before the park trails were built, the old trail—beaten path is a more accurate description—passed a few hundred yards to the north of this spectacular display of water, and we didn't know there was any such thing as Ramsey Cascades. Now it is the destination of many hikes. Before the breathtaking trail was built around the Tennessee side of Charlies Bunion, the old path swung along the more gentle slopes of the North Carolina side with the result that hikers of those days knew nothing of the views now enjoyed at "the Bunion."

For those who prefer wilderness hiking, there are hundreds and hundreds of miles of streams and ridges with no trail whatsoever. Three-fourths of the park's area is, and will remain, as wilderness. This provides more opportunities for wilderness hiking than can be covered in a normal lifetime. In these rugged areas the hiker can still have the thrill of getting lost by making the wrong turn at the forks of a stream, or by descending the wrong ridge. Ours is a big park, with areas and facilities to serve the needs or wishes of visitors having a great variety of preferences.

There is no agreement as to what caused the grassy balds of the Great Smokies. There is, however, plenty of evidence that prepark grazing served to prevent any possible forest intrusion on these mountaintop meadows. There is also evidence that during prepark years grass was gradually replacing trees along much of the Great Smokies crest. Grazing cattle and sheep nipped off the young oak and beech sprouts when they were only a few inches high. After many years, this left an open stand of more or less mature trees, with no young trees to replace the old ones that died or were blown down by strong winds. Hundreds of hikers can recall the parklike appearance of the main crest just east of Gregory Bald and just above the famous Moores Spring. There was plenty of grass but no underbrush. As grazing stopped, when the land was taken over by the park, there was soon a dense stand of young trees where there had been lush growths of grasses.

It is my belief that if grazing had been continued for another fifty or one hundred years there would have been a continuous grassy bald all the way from Gregory Bald to Thunderhead, a distance of almost twelve miles.

Two of these "meadows in the sky" were not known as Balds, but as "fields." These are Spence Field, just west of Thunderhead, and Russell Field, a few more miles to the west. There is good evidence that both of these fields were cleared. In fact, large numbers of stumps from the clearing were still standing in Russell Field long after the hiking club was organized.

Although Spence Field was cleared much earlier, I have talked with two men who reported personal knowledge of forest cover on Spence Field.

In 1936 Dan Myers of Cades Cove, who was then eighty-three years old, told my daughter (Mrs. H. C. Harvey, Jr.) and me that he made his first trip to the Spence Field area in 1869, when he was sixteen years old. He told us that it was then a forest made up mostly of beech trees.

In March 1967 Charles S. Dunn of Dry Valley, who was a former chief ranger for the Great Smokies, told me that Bob Spence of White Oak Cove—near Schoolhouse Gap—had cleared Spence Field with the help of Ike Patty in about 1870. This was done to provide more mountaintop grazing land for their cattle. Mr. Dunn said that they first girdled the buckeye trees to kill them so the cattle would not be poisoned by eating the buckeyes. Although the buckeye trees and many others were cut later, it was never a general clearing—such as would have been needed for cultivation. A number of scattered trees were left for shade. The purpose of the clearing of Spence Field, he said, was not for cultivation, but just to provide more grazing land for his cattle. Mr. Dunn told me that he saw several tree stumps remaining in Spence Field as late as 1906.

The summer of 1936 was the last time that grazing was permitted at Spence Field. Some years later, with cattle not there to eat the trees just after they sprouted, a few young trees began to fight their way up through the dense stand of tall grass. By 1967 there was a considerable number of trees from ten to twenty-five feet tall scattered throughout Spence Field. Grazing had continued on Gregory Bald until 1936.

Bob Spence, for whom Spence Field was named, also left his name on at least one other field. That is implied by the fact that a small stream just a short distance west of the Schoolhouse Gap Road or old Anderson Road has been known as "Spence Deadening Branch." A "deadening" is a new field, usually called "newground," in which the trees have been killed by girdling—the removal of about two or three feet of the bark all around the trees. After a crop was made the dead trees were removed, usually during the following winter.

Mr. Dunn also told me that there is a small area on Miry Ridge, southwest of Elkmont, that was formerly known as Mike's Deadening. It appears, therefore, that the girdling of trees, preliminary to a later clearing, might have been a general practice in the mountain foothills. It would, in many cases, permit the farmer to get a crop one year earlier than would have been possible if there had been the necessity for a general clearing before the first crop was planted.

Early hikers to Silers Bald found a grassy meadow covering a few acres on the very summit, along with a grassy meadow of perhaps as much as twenty-five acres along the crest of Welch Ridge, which extended downward on the North Carolina side of Silers. Grazing was discontinued on Silers several years before it was stopped on Gregory Bald. As a result, the beech forest quickly started encroaching on the western side of the summit. As far back as 1940 the young beech trees, then from ten to twenty feet tall, had crowded up to within a few feet of the crest. At the same time, a low-growing species of blackberry had crowded out most of the grass along the upper end of Welch Ridge. Thus, most of Silers Bald had succumbed to the encroachment by about 1940, leaving very little grass on that once beautiful bald. Most of the remaining grass was on the very steep slope on the eastern edge of Silers. This, however, still preserved the superb view of Clingmans Dome and other peaks and ridges between Clingmans and Mt. LeConte.

Nature's Sand Factory

It may come as a surprise to some people to learn that one of the world's oldest manufacturing "plants" is in full operation in the Great Smokies.

It is an endless process, which runs day and night, 365 days per year, with no holidays or vacations. And it follows the efficient practice used in other kinds of manufacturing plants—that of starting the process at or near the top, then working downward until the finished product comes out at the bottom.

The next time you are at the edge of a rocky promontory in the Great Smokies, please take a close look at the apparently solid rock. Most likely you will see small, or even larger, crevices here and there in the rock. When it rains some of the water runs into those crevices, of course. And on cold winter days the water in the crevices will freeze. As the water turns to ice there is a swelling action that soon enlarges the crevices a small fraction of an inch. This makes more room for the water during following rains, and the swelling action when that water freezes becomes more powerful and pushes the rocks still farther apart. After countless repetitions, a piece of rock—sometimes very small and sometimes quite large—is sent tumbling down the steep cliffs. That is the first phase of this age-old manufacturing process.

Each time the falling rock—or maybe it's a small boulder—strikes other rocks, some of the sharp edges are broken off. Some of those rocks may lie at their first landing spot for many years, even decades, or centuries, until a rain of cloudburst proportions carries them farther down the side of the mountain—again knocking off more of the sharp edges. Although it may take hundreds or thousands of years to do it, many of those rocks are washed into the swirling mountain streams. There they are rolled along a few feet more with each period of high water, finally winding up as rounded stones, which are usually known as river rocks.

You may ask, "What happens to all of those tiny sharp edges that were knocked off as the original stone broke loose from the cliff and started on its course down the mountain?" Well, they eventually find their way into the rivers of the valleys, where they are scooped up by the dredges operated by sand companies.

The process just described, as you have possibly already surmised, is "Nature's sand factory," one of the world's oldest manufacturing plants.

LOOKING AND SEEING

On one trip while hiking between Low Gap and Mt. Cammerer (then White Rock), I had stopped to make a picture of beech drops, an interesting but little-known plant that grows only from the roots of beech trees. As will be seen in a moment, it is appropriate that I mention the fact that I was wearing lace-legged khaki trousers and boots that reached almost to my knees.

While getting set up to make the picture, Tom Duncan, one of the other hikers of my group stopped to watch and to ask the identity of the plant.

After giving him the name, I told him that I might have assumed that the trees nearby were yellow birches if I had not seen the beech drops. I then reminded him that the two species of trees are somewhat similar in appearance. "I guess I know one from the other," I observed, "but I'm not sure that I could explain the differences so anyone else would be able to make the distinction."

"If you really know the difference," Tom said, "you should be able to tell others what it is."

"I'm not so sure of that," I replied. "I happen to know that Henry Duncan is farther out the trail. We are close to the same age, and about the same build, if, then, someone wanted to see a certain one of us, and wanted to be sure to approach the correct one, how would you tell him which is which?"

Much quicker than is required to tell it, Tom's very observant answer was "I'd tell him that the man with the *straight* legs is Duncan."

A botanist friend insists, with good reason, that most people do a lot of looking but very little seeing. This experience of some forty years ago caused me at least to try to do a little more *seeing* along with a lot of *looking*.

🖉   🖉   🖉

After I had climbed Mt. LeConte more than fifty times—later increased to more than eighty times—my wife asked why I went to LeConte so often. I told her that I was pretty certain that I had seen or learned something new on each and every trip.

Some months later she was with me on another LeConte hike. While we were eating our lunch, just below Rainbow Falls, she recalled my answer and told me that she was going to check up on me by seeing what, if anything, I learned on this particular trip. Naturally, I was a bit fearful that this might just be the time when I didn't see anything new. But it must have been my lucky day. Before we started back down the mountain, I had listed two new "finds" and several weeks later added a third new bit of information from the trip.

About halfway up the mountain I saw some odd-looking gooseberries. Each berry had several short, soft spines, which I suspected to be the result of insect stings or some other such cause. So I collected several berries with the intention of taking them to the University of Tennessee Department of Botany to see what had caused the spines. But I didn't have to wait that long. While we were resting and enjoying the sweeping panorama from Cliff Top, I heard noises in the shrubs that grew on the extremely steep cliff below us. In a few minutes we learned that we had heard Dr. Stanley A. Cain, then professor of botany at the University of Tennessee, who was exploring the various plants that were growing on the face of Cliff Top. When I showed the "diseased" gooseberries to him, he immediately described them as natural growths that were peculiar to that species of gooseberry, and not caused by disease or injury. He identified the species as *Ribes cynosbati,* commonly known as "Dogberry," or "prickly gooseberry." That information alone saved the day for me, but it was not the end.

While scanning the views from our Cliff Top vantage point, I saw a previously unnoticed peak looming conspicuously on the skyline to the southwest. It must have been the character of the light that made the peak stand out so plainly whereas I had never before "seen" it. After looking closely at the location, I could see that it was on Welch Ridge, which extends down into North Carolina from Silers Bald, apparently in the general vicinity of what was then the park line. The only peak in that location that I had known about was Welch Bald, and for a time I supposed it to be Welch Bald. On checking my maps, I discovered the interesting peak was designated as High Rocks, but I had never before even heard that name, much less known the location.

With an elevation of 5,188 feet above sea level, High Rocks is higher than Newfound Gap (5,045); Mt. Cammerer (5,025), then known as White Rock; and Gregory Bald (4,948). This, then, became the second "new thing" I had seen on this hike, during which Mrs. Campbell was checking up on me.

Knowledge of the third new thing didn't come to light until some weeks later, but it was on that day that Dr. Cain found a species of grass that, up to that time, was unknown to science. It was growing on the steep west face of Cliff Top and was found as Dr. Cain crawled up through the dense vegetation. Not being familiar with the species, Dr. Cain sent a sample to the nation's leading authority on grasses. It was verified as an entirely new species and was named, by the grass specialist, in honor of Dr. Cain. The name is *Calamagrostis cainii,* with the common name of "Cain's reed grass."

With such a record of new things learned on a single trip, I decided to "quit while I was ahead," although I still do see or learn new things quite frequently.

✐   ✐   ✐

An alert hiker can sometimes find interesting information about a specific location in the mountains, just by "reading" nature's message.

Myron H. Avery, the dynamic leader of the Appalachian Trail development, gave a good illustration of this fact. Some time after his first visit to Clingmans Dome—which, incidentally, is the highest point on the entire Appalachian Trail, elevation 6,643 feet—he asked me when the summit of the dome had been cleared.

"It has never been cleared," I told him. "Don't you remember that there is a dense stand of tall trees, mostly balsam [Fraser fir]?"

"Yes, I know that the whole mountaintop is forested," he replied, "but the next time you are there just take a look at the size, or ages, of the trees in a radius of about fifty or seventy-five feet around the tower. You will see that all of them are comparatively young. Beyond that point you will see trees of various ages or sizes, some of which are much older than any tree in the inner circle."

This fact I had never noticed. On my next visit I checked and found that Myron had been able to read an interesting story by his practice of keeping his eyes open when in the mountains—and from this I learned a valuable lesson.

By applying the same principles, I was able to see for myself that the beautiful open meadow at Indian Gap had been made by clearing the trees. I reached that conclusion by noting that all of the several nearby "gaps" were still covered by trees and shrubs. I reasoned that if Indian Gap had been a natural mountaintop meadow at least some of the other little gaps should have been open meadows also.

A little later, during a conversation with the late general Frank Maloney, I told him that it was my opinion, based on what I had seen in the area, that Indian Gap had been cleared by man.

"That's correct," General Maloney said. "In 1896 I spent two weeks hiking and camping in the general vicinity of Indian Gap. My companions and helpers were Steve Cole and Vance Newman, who lived in the Sugarlands. While we were camped in Indian Gap, I heard them talk of hearing their fathers tell of the building of the old Indian Gap road. They reported that the Indians who built the road had cleared a few acres in the gap so they could establish a construction camp, with stables for their mules."

Thus, General Maloney was able to verify my feeble effort at reading nature's message.

Arthur Stupka, former park chief naturalist, gave another interesting example of reading nature. While we were resting at Alum Cave Bluff, I noticed a somewhat unusual arrangement of the branches of a red spruce tree that was growing just under the edge of the overhanging bluff. Contrary to what we expected, the branches reaching in toward the wall of the bluff were four or five times as long as those that reached out toward the light. And all of the shorter branches were about the same length—about three or four feet.

Mr. Stupka, who had "read the story from nature" told us that the ends of outer branches, being directly under the overhang, received a new "haircut" several times each winter when icicles fell while the branches were rigid from the cold weather. The falling icicles thus clipped off the end of any branch that had grown enough to get into the path of the icicle.

In the mountains, as elsewhere, a great variety of sounds may be heard almost continuously. There is the soft rustling of the trees as their branches are swayed by the gentle winds, or the roar from stronger winds. There are the musical sounds made by the water as it tumbles over ledges or boulders in its course down the steep mountainsides. There are the songs of birds by day, and the songs of crickets and other insects—and the occasional hooting of an owl, or the cry of a bobcat, by night. And, around a cheerful campfire, there is the popping of the fire and the conversation of the campers.

An exception to this pattern was noted several years ago by Herbert M. Webster and two camping friends near the top of Mt. Guyot, while they were resting between the evening meal and retiring. Herbert, with whom I have had many fine hikes, reported that during a lull in their conversation there was something about the situation that he could not understand at first, and he learned later that his companions had also noticed it. Pretty soon, however, they realized that they had experienced a period of what seemed to be complete silence. They didn't have a campfire, there was no perceptible wind, they were not within hearing distance of any stream, and there were no birds, crickets, or other insects to be heard.

"The silence was quite impressive as well as unusual," he said.

Another case of impressive mountaintop silence, though temporarily interrupted, occurred on Myrtle Point of Mt. LeConte while members of the Smoky Mountains Hiking Club were awaiting the sunrise. In the group was a visitor who had been brought by one of the members.

The setting was just right for a glorious experience. A sea of clouds filled the deep gorge below us, and there were a few scattered clouds in the eastern sky. Early touches of red let us know that it was to be an unusually colorful spectacle.

Everyone was appropriately quiet—some, no doubt, offering prayers of thanks for the privilege of seeing such a thrilling sight. Then, as that big ball of fire began to rise over the distant mountains, we were startled to hear four or five pistol shots shatter the erstwhile silence. We quickly saw that the visitor was the offender.

It was both surprising and highly pleasing to see that not a single word was said to him, and I'm sure that our silence was a much sharper reprimand than if we had complained to him. As evidence that he learned his lesson, he made abject apologies to many of us during the next several days. "Somehow or other I just thought that it was the thing to do, but I see that I was very wrong," he said. He later joined the hiking club and became a good member.

These two vastly different experiences illustrate the fact that there are many occasions when there is a solemnity to silence.

Most of my preparations had been made for an overnight hike, but I still had to purchase a few packaged food items. On a Saturday morning, when I stopped at the neighborhood store to make these purchases, I was wearing hiking clothing and carrying my pack, thus making it very clear where I was headed.

In the store I was greeted by a neighbor and good friend, Dr. C. O. Sherbakoff, a renowned University of Tennessee plant pathologist. He commented that I must be starting on a two-day hike. Then, much to my surprise, he proceeded to lecture me on the evils of Sunday hiking. To use a slang expression, he really "poured it on!"

I'll have to admit that I did a bit of squirming as I sought to defend myself. He listened attentively, but with some evidence of skepticism, as I told him about the inspirational and spiritual values I had gotten while standing on a lofty mountaintop, surveying the sea of clouds that spread endlessly before me. I told him that there is, indeed, a powerful "sermon" in watching an indescribably beautiful sunrise or sunset from a rugged vantage point. I reminded him that one is deeply impressed by the intricate patterns of various wildflowers, and that one gets a feeling of overpowering humility while admiring the stately giants in a primeval forest.

Then, with a wry smile on his face, and with his delightful dialect that we had learned to enjoy, Dr. Sherbakoff said, "Oh, I vas just a bit envious!"

As stated previously, during the early days of the park movement we sought to get every prominent visitor into the park area and especially to the top of Mt. LeConte. The admitted purpose of this hospitality was the hope of getting those visitors to help promote the park movement in every way possible, particularly with publicity.

On one occasion I invited Dr. Hight C. Moore, an official of the Tennessee Baptist Association and editor of the denomination's Sunday school publication *Kind Words,* to climb Mt. LeConte with me. He accepted, and we had a delightful trip.

As we sat at the top of Rainbow Falls, eating our lunch, there was a beautiful display of purple rhododendron near the edge of the precipice. Dr. Moore called attention to the fact that a cluster of the colorful flowers reached over the edge of the stream and was being swept back and forth as each wave of the water caught the flower. This interplay of the flower and the water continued the whole time we were there.

When he returned to his Nashville office, Dr. Moore wrote an interesting account of this trip, and it was published in an early issue of *Kind Words*. The only detail of his article that I can now recall was the effective manner in which he described the continuous contact of the rhododendron and the water. He told of our enjoyment in "watching the rhododendron as it leaned over to kiss the water just before it made the leap over the waterfall."

∅   ∅   ∅

Following a meeting of the Appalachian Trail Conference at Gatlinburg, I climbed Mt. LeConte with about forty members of the Potomac Appalachian Trail Club and the Mountain Club of Maryland. It was a cloudy day and rain was expected.

After resting a while at LeConte Lodge, we went out to Cliff Top to await the sunset. The clouds were approximately one thousand feet above us as we climbed the old prepark wooden tower that was still standing on Cliff Top. Our visibility was exceptionally good as the clouds filtered out the glare we might have had—somewhat like holding your hands over your eyes to enable you to get a better view of the distant points.

In about thirty minutes we spotted what seemed to be an approaching storm. It was hovering over Cades Cove, which on clear days is visible from Cliff Top. Soon we heard the rumbling of distant thunder and could see occasional flashes of lightning in the Cades Cove area. At first we could still see Rich Mountain, but not for long. The clouds were moving eastward, straight toward Mt. LeConte.

As the storm came closer, we could still see Blanket Mountain, but here again it was for only a short time. The thunder became sharper and more frequent as it approached, and it was obvious that we were to be drenched in a very few minutes.

About that time the overhead clouds moved on farther to the east, and we had the treat of seeing a peculiarly bright copper-colored sky off to the right (northwest). It appeared very much as though the sky was composed of molten metal. By that time most of the hikers had already descended from the tower and were watching from the greater safety of the ground. One of the most fascinating sights I ever witnessed was watching the last two hikers as they climbed down the rustic steps that had been nailed to a corner support of the observation platform. Silhouetted against that sky of molten copper, they gave us a strange, eerie sight.

Had the scene been less dramatic, most of the group would have gone back to the shelter of the lodge before the storm struck LeConte. But it would have been difficult to walk out on such a thrilling and unusual show.

The result was that most, if not all, of us were still on Cliff Top as the storm moved across and obliterated the view of Chimney Tops. Lightning was then flashing sharply almost directly below us, and five minutes later we felt the full burst of the rain. We were, of course, quickly drenched to the skin—since most of us had not bothered to take rain gear to Cliff Top with us.

With the wet clothing sticking closely to our bodies, we were plenty cold before we reached the lodge. But it was a very low price to pay for such a rare and long-to-be-remembered treat.

People of the Mountains

Restricted World

In prepark days people living in the Great Smokies and the surrounding mountains did very little traveling. It was not unusual for a man or woman to live and die in the immediate community, perhaps in the same house, where they were born. Many of them never traveled more than ten or fifteen miles from their homes. And a man who had gone as much as one hundred miles from his place of birth was regarded as a real traveler. Most of them led extremely restricted lives.

On my first hike down the south side of Mt. LeConte, by way of Alum Cave Bluff, I saw a little boy about six or seven years old standing in the trail. He was watching in amazement the big group of, to him, strangely dressed men and women. His home, on the site of the present Chimneys Campground, was just across the river from us. When I asked who lived in the house, his reply was "Mommy."

It was quite obvious that to him "Mommy" was one of the most important people in the world. Anybody and everybody should know "Mommy," he seemed to imply. A few weeks later I got to wondering why "Poppy" didn't also live there. Upon inquiry I learned that his father had lost his life in an accident. That, of course, made "Mommy" an even more important person in his young life.

In thinking back over this incident, I recalled a slightly similar situation about which I had read in Margaret Morley's book *Carolina Mountains*. She told about a mountain woman whose world was also very small, and who had just learned that in 1904 a World's Fair was being held in St. Louis, a city about which she had never heard. To her it might just as well been on the other side of the world.

"I don't see why they didn't have it here in Asheville so everybody could get there," she said.

Yes, the early settlers did live pretty much unto themselves. But, with the advent of a network of good roads throughout the mountains, all of that has been changed and most of the mountain people do now get to travel a bit.

THE WALKER SISTERS

In September of 1937, Miss Evelyn Kappes, a Knoxville woman who was working on her master's degree at the University of Michigan, came to me for suggestions as to where and how she could get some firsthand information about games that had been played by mountain children, especially in the Great Smokies. I gave her the names of several mountain friends who might be able to provide the desired information, and found her to be particularly interested in the famed and self-reliant Walker sisters. They were five spinster sisters who then had lived together for many years, doing all of their own farming and housework.

Miss Kappes was not familiar with the Little River Gorge section of the Smokies, near which the sisters lived, and I realized that it would be next to impossible to give directions that would enable her to find their home. So I volunteered to take her to see them.

When we arrived at the famous home, about 10:30 or 11 A.M., we saw that they had company—a married sister and three or four other relatives who were there for the midday dinner. We were greeted cordially enough, but it was easy to see that they were preoccupied with their company and that it would be difficult or impossible to get any information until after the family had eaten. Also there at the time was Warner Ogden, a newspaper writer and photographer who was making no progress whatever in his efforts to get pictures of the famous sisters. Realizing that his chances for a picture were extremely slim, he left in a short time. Miss Kappes and I, however, were still hopeful, and were in no hurry to leave.

Though they discouraged my efforts to get pictures on the pretext that Margaret, the oldest sister, had a "sick headache," they did invite us to have dinner with them. But they said that we would have to eat at the second table—there being far too many people for all to eat at the same time.

There were no screens on the doors or windows, and it was necessary to use the "fly-brush" to keep the flies away from the table while the meal was being eaten. Most mountain families used a very simple fly-brush, in some cases just a branch from a tree and in most cases a long, slender piece of newspaper tacked to a strip of wood, with the paper cut into narrow strips. The brushes were swung back and forth across the table throughout the entire meal.

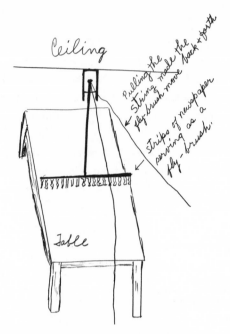

Ceiling

Pulling the the
String made the
fly-brush move back + forth

Strips of newspaper
serving as a
fly-brush.

Table

Sketch of a "fly-brush," used to keep
insects away from the table during meals.

The Walker sisters, September 1, 1937. Left to right: Hettie, Louisa,
Martha, Polly and Margaret.

In the Walker home, however, the fly-brush was quite a bit more complicated, and more effective. A vertical piece of slender wood was suspended from the ceiling, with about a foot-long portion extending above the crosspiece that supported it. This left a section of the wooden strip, some four or five feet long, hanging below the supporting crossbar. At the lower end of this there was a fly-brush that extended from one side of the table to the other. A string tied to the upper end of the vertical support permitted it to be pulled back and forth lengthwise above the table. The accompanying sketch will doubtless give a much better idea of how the device worked.

Still hopeful of getting some pictures as well as information about childhood games, I volunteered to sit in the open doorway to the dining room and operate the fly-brush while those at the first table were eating. To my surprise, my invitation was accepted, and I became the "fly-shooer." This gesture of friendship on my part seemed to make us, Miss Kappes and me, almost members of the family. They talked more freely, and we soon learned that although most mountain children did play a variety of games, the childhood days of these frugal and industrious sisters were so busily filled with work that "we had no time for playing games," they confided.

After the table was cleared of dishes from the "first table," two of the sisters, Miss Kappes, and I then became the "second table," as some other member of the family operated the fly-brush. Interestingly enough, we had an excellent and varied meal.

As I finished eating, I again inquired of Margaret about the state of her health. She admitted that she felt much better since having eaten.

"This, then, would be a good time to make some pictures," I suggested hopefully, "wouldn't it?"

To my surprise and pleasure, she agreed to permit the picture making, as did the four other sisters. They then posed freely, and as many times as I requested. I first made two shots of all five, standing in a row from oldest to youngest. This was then repeated with all of them seated. After that, I was permitted to make separate pictures, each showing some favorite activity of the particular sister that was being photographed. Louisa, the poet of the family, posed with one of her poems in her hand. Margaret, who was an expert quilt maker, posed beside one of her most beautiful quilts. Another, Polly I believe it was, posed at the nearby spring.

When, a few weeks later, I sent prints of the pictures to them, I volunteered to give them enlargements of any that they especially liked. On October 11, 1937, they wrote me a letter in which they expressed appreciation and gave me the identification of four or five pictures for which they asked enlargements.

I'm sure there is a lesson in this true story. Part of it is that it doesn't pay to try to rush mountain people into doing anything, especially something about which they are already a bit skeptical. I'm equally sure that the time I spent pulling the string to that ingenious fly-brush is what turned the trick in my favor, so soon after they had given a completely cold shoulder to the newspaper photographer.

Although Witt Shields was not one of the most publicized residents of Cades Cove, he was a progressive and public-spirited citizen. He lived on the south side of the cove, just off the newly relocated road on the return part of the eleven-mile loop. His father was Henry Shields, one of the very earliest settlers—possibly the second or third. Witt Shields died in 1918, at which time he was approximately seventy years old. Interesting information about him was given to me in 1955 by his grandson, Lester Shields.

An indication of his resourcefulness and progressive qualities is seen in the fact that, in about 1915, he built a water line about half a mile long, from a good spring down to his two-story frame house. This not merely furnished fresh running water for his general use, but also provided a degree of "refrigeration." He built a wooden open-topped box, about ten feet long and fifteen inches wide, through which the cold springwater ran continuously. At the upper end the box was only about three inches deep and about two feet long, for use in storing butter and other small items of food that needed to be kept cool. The next section of about five feet was approximately six inches deep, in which somewhat larger containers were placed. At the lower edge of the box the water was deep enough for storing crocks of milk and other bulky items.

This water was made to do double duty; what otherwise would have been an overflow was piped off just below the top level and carried through additional pipes to the barnyard for use of the cattle and horses. A branch line from this gravity water system was also extended about a mile and a half to the Consolidated School, a two-story school near the Primitive Baptist Church. This, insofar as I have been able to learn, is the only gravity water system and cooling device in the cove. It was a common practice to store milk, butter, and similar items at the springs near many of the homes.

His public-spirited nature was shown in several ways, one of which was his practice of making caskets of seasoned solid walnut lumber for neighbors who died—and to do so without any charge. Lester told that in numerous cases the first time his grandfather knew about a recent death was when he saw a man walking down the road, carrying a long stick to show how tall the deceased person was. A generous supply of solid walnut lumber for this purpose was stored on the open joists of his workshop.

Despite the fact that Witt Shields had established himself as a good neighbor in the community, he occasionally found evidence that some person had been stealing corn from his well-stocked crib. Although he kept the crib door locked, the thief had gotten into the crib by climbing up the slatted side of the crib and going in from above. To meet this situation, Mr. Shields got a good-sized steel trap, wrapped the strong jaws of the trap with rags so it would not cripple anyone who might get caught in it, then set the trap inside the crib where the thief had been entering. It worked, and a young neighbor was caught and held fast until released.

When Mr. Shields learned that the young man's family was in need, he told the thief to shuck enough of the corn for a "turn" at the mill, and allowed him to pay for it by chopping some wood for Mr. Shields. And he did not prosecute the corn taker, but told him that anytime his family was in need for cornmeal he should come to Mr. Shields for more corn on the basis of working to pay for it.

Once, when squirrels were found to be raiding the corn crib, Mr. Shields drilled a hole through a walnut and fastened one end of a wire to the walnut and the other end to a trigger that would release a trap enclosure. In this manner he caught several squirrels, which the family ate, and also broke up another "ring" of corn thieves.

WALL OF IGNORANCE

Prior to 1912 several women from the national fraternity Pi Beta Phi rode horseback into Gatlinburg, where they hoped to enlist cooperation for their plan to teach handicrafts and public health as well as the three R's. They had been conducting a survey of various foothill communities where the fraternity might establish such a settlement school. At the end of the survey it selected Gatlinburg as the logical community for the school.

In their effort to ascertain the amount of local cooperation they might expect, members of the committee found many who wanted the school, but some of the larger landowners were less than enthusiastic about the plan. Being definitely orthodox in their religious thinking, they expressed fears that some "dangerous doctrines" might also be taught, and they opposed the school. Since the visiting women were unable to find anyone who would donate the necessary land, they decided to abandon the idea of establishing the school at Gatlinburg. Early the following morning they mounted the horses they were to ride back to Pigeon Forge and Sevierville. At that time it was difficult to reach Gatlinburg except by horseback.

But something else happened during the night before the Pi Phi women rode away. Martha Jane Huff, the first wife of Andrew Jackson Huff, the founder and owner of the Mountain View Hotel, had a dream that disturbed her very much. She called her husband and told him about the dream, in which she had seen a black wall of water sweeping down the mountainside. She interpreted the dream to mean that it was a "wall of ignorance" that was about to engulf her two sons and three daughters.

In response to Martha Jane's urgent request, Andy quickly mounted his own horse and rode as fast as he could until he overtook the departing women. He told them that if they would return with him, he would see to it that a suitable school site was made available to them. They did return, and the school was established.

Such was the beginning of Gatlinburg's famous "Pi Phi" School which did so much to make Gatlinburg one of the most progressive communities in or near the Great Smokies. Thousands of children who went to school there, and large numbers of adults who were trained in various handcrafts or who were helped by the public health program of the school, owe debts of gratitude to Martha Jane and Andy Huff.

WHISKEY MAKING

Although the Cosby section gets credit, or blame, for having the most moonshine stills (distilleries) of any section of the Great Smokies, it is a known fact that the illicit manufacturing of whiskey was practiced to some extent in all parts of the foothills region. Many men who were otherwise law-abiding citizens would argue that it was their corn and that they had a right to do with it whatever they wanted. Some even argued that it was just about the only practical way they had of getting their corn "to the market." And most of the moonshiners would sincerely argue that the government had no right to tax their whiskey. Except for the few years during which the Volstead Act was a law, there was no law against making whiskey. Their real problem was to get it made and sold without having to pay the tax.

Despite the reputed widespread operation of moonshine stills throughout the foothills of the Smokies, I have seen only one still in my more than forty years of hiking, and that one was in full operation. It not only was not in the Cosby section but was not even very close to what is now the park border. The hiking club was conducting a hike to English Mountain, several miles north of Cosby. On previous club hikes to this interesting destination we had gone up and back by the same graded trail, then westward along the crest to the fire tower and on to the spectacular cliffs a short distance farther along.

While eating our lunches and enjoying the views from atop those rugged cliffs, a small number of us decided to return by a different route, for which there was no trail. We just went down the mountainside, through the forest, until we reached a small stream and then followed the stream because we realized that it would lead us directly to our cars at Carson Springs. We were walking quietly, with little or no conversation at the moment. To our great surprise we saw a small group of men across the stream, and the wisps of smoke that rose from nearby disclosed for us the nature of their activities. Because our approach was so nearly noiseless, we were almost directly opposite them before they saw us.

Realizing that this was no time for socializing, I managed to get out a feeble "howdy" as we walked on by, trying hard to leave the appearance that we did not know what they were doing.

For several days afterward I read the newspapers carefully to see if I could learn whether or not the "revenooers" had found that still, but never did find any reference to any such result.

Not all of the whiskey and other alcoholic beverages made in what is now park lands was of the illicit kind, however. It has come as a surprise to many newcomers to these mountains to learn that in and near Cades Cove there were two legal distilleries in operation before and shortly after the turn of the century.

Information on the subject was passed on to me by Dr. A. Randolph Shields, head of the Department of Biology of Maryville College and a native of Cades Cove, and by A. J. Fisher, of Maryville, who spent many years exploring the mountains around Cades Cove and also served as super-intendent of the Civilian Conservation Corps Camp in Cades Cove during the mid-1930s. These men, and others, report that Jule Gregg operated a government-licensed distillery in the southwest corner of Cades Cove, and that his product was government bonded and taxed.

They also report George W. Powell operated another bonded distillery about three miles west of Cades Cove, on the old Parsons Branch Road. The Powell distillery not only made corn whiskey but also made large quantities of apple brandy, hence the lingering remnants of the old apple orchard. Both of these distilleries bottled their liquors, paid the government taxes on it, and sold most of it at the still.

Charlie Myers, a native of the cove who for several years was one of the operators of the reactivated John P. Cable grist mill, told me in 1967 that although both the Gregg and Powell distilleries were government "bonded" operations, it was generally understood in the Cove that unstamped whiskey could also be bought, at a lower price, by people well known to the owners. Mr. Myers said that the Powell Distillery went out of business about 1900, and that the Gregg operation ceased about 1904.

In addition to the two legal distilleries, Mr. Fisher told that there were also "oodles" of moonshine stills in and around the cove.

WEATHER

VARIETY IN WEATHER

Weather in the Great Smoky Mountains National Park differs widely from that in the surrounding valleys. Not merely is it different, but the variations often are contrary to what may have been expected. This is especially true with reference to temperatures. Although weather is a major influence affecting one's enjoyment of trips into the Smokies, very little specific information has been available.

I have spent the night on Mt. LeConte when the unofficial temperature was twenty degrees below zero. It was zero in nearby Knoxville. On the other extreme, I have rested in shirtsleeves and in perfect comfort on the same Mt. LeConte in December and January. I have been in cloudbursts, and I have seen the mountains so dry, and for such a long time, that many trees actually died of thirst. I have hiked in the rain much of the day, then had the thrill of watching the clouds dramatically roll away through the deep-cut gorges. I have stood on mountain peaks and looked out across a veritable sea of sunlit clouds, with other mountaintops appearing much like islands jutting up out of an ocean. I have watched the dramatic approach of a storm, with lightning flashing in the gorges below me. Fortunately for me, I have not been in a severe windstorm, but I have seen many of the blow-downs that remain as mute evidence of the fact that occasional such storms have been there. I have hiked in knee-deep snows, and I have seen flowers blooming in the mountains every month of the year, sometimes with remnants of snow within a foot or so.

Such casual observations as these made by hikers over a period of years were about all that was known of the Great Smokies weather until the early 1930s. It is only natural, therefore, that I should have wondered: How often may these conditions be expected? To what extent are they normal, or abnormal? Also, it is natural that I wished to see weather-recording instruments installed—and tried to get them installed—so that the answers to these and other questions could be made available.

The first step was made in 1934, when the Hydraulic Data Division of the Tennessee Valley Authority (TVA) installed automatic reporting rain gauges on Clingmans Dome and at other points in and near the Great Smokies. The next step came in 1939, when National Park Service road crews started making surface measurements of snowfall at Newfound Gap and at other points on the transmountain highway.

Temperature and relative humidity studies were not started until December 1945. This was done through the cooperation of the National Park Service, TVA's Hydraulic Data Division, and the U.S. Weather Bureau. Scientific snow gauges were installed at seven points along the transmountain highway, and automatic recording hygrothermographs were installed at four of these same points. A later station was added at the end of the road on Forney Ridge, elevation 6,310 feet, near the 6,643-foot summit of Clingmans Dome. Since readings from the latter station are not available during winter months, the highest elevation used in my temperature studies is from the 5,045-foot Newfound Gap, where the transmountain road crosses the crest of the Smokies. Gatlinburg, the park headquarters village, and Knoxville have been included for comparisons.

◇ ◇ ◇

Those who have been in the higher elevations of the Smokies, particularly at Collins Gap on Clingmans Dome Road, when the sunlit hoarfrost covers every twig, have experienced a real thrill. It is one of the most dazzlingly beautiful sights that it has been my good fortune to see. In my opinion it far surpasses the beauty of the June and July displays of rhododendron and the autumnal color spectacles. "Fairyland" is the term most often used in efforts to describe the exquisite beauty of hoarfrost.

"Frozen fog," as hoarfrost is called by most of the mountain people, is formed when the clouds are down on the mountains and the temperature is below the freezing point. As the particles of moisture in the clouds touch a frozen twig or other object, they are transformed into tiny ice crystals. If there is little or no wind, as is usually the case in the deep forests, the ice crystals form on all sides of the twig. But when there is a fairly strong wind, the ice forms only on the windward side and soon creates "needles of ice" that project out into the wind. An imaginative friend refers to these as "angel feathers."

On clear days people in the valleys have been heard to call the attention of friends to the "snow on top of the Smokies." Most likely, however, what they saw was not snow but hoarfrost, or a combination of the two.

The same winds that blow away the snow clouds serve also to blow most of the snow from the tree branches. When seen from a fairly close range this presents a cold, gray effect—mostly bare tree branches with a ground cover of snow as a background. Hoarfrost, however, sticks tightly to the twigs and tree branches and, produces a dazzling coat of pure white that completely

145

Hoarfrost (frozen fog) on birch tree in Collins Gap creates a dazzlingly beautiful sight, April 11, 1937.

covers the mountaintops. When it is only snow on the mountain the visible effect is much less attractive. When it is hoarfrost, or a combination of frost and snow, the result is a glistening coat, the beauty and glamour of which defies description.

Every wintertime visitor to the Great Smokies should drive to the top of the mountain when the hoarfrost forms, or even when the snows fall. You may ask, "How about the roads? Aren't they dangerous?"

When snow starts falling in the Smokies the park road crews begin to clear the roads and to spread cinders or sand on the icy portions. As a rule, after a general snowfall, the safest driving from Knoxville to the Smokies is that between Gatlinburg and the top of the mountain. When, on rare occasions, the road crews can't keep the snow removed as fast as it falls; the road is closed for short periods. At times the use of tire chains is required, and the regulation is enforced rigidly! The roads are posted clearly when chains are required. At other times, with careful driving, the roads are safe—and the brave motorists are given a treat.

Even so, there will be times when park roads can not be cleared as rapidly as would be desired, especially when heavy snows are still falling. When there is an accumulation of snow on the road, it is unsafe to drive on such a road unless the car is equipped with tire chains. Even with chains, a car can skid out of control while negotiating a curve or while meeting or trying to pass another vehicle. One death occurred and another was barely averted on February 23, 1947, when the road through Little River Gorge (Tennessee Highway #73) was covered with about six or more inches of snow, and more still falling.

Mrs. Bonaventura Spink Cuniff and her sister, Dr. Urbana Spink, both of Indianapolis, Indiana, entered the park near Townsend, with Gatlinburg as their destination. When only four miles from Townsend their car skidded off the pavement. Since they could not get the car back on the road, the two ladies—both in their sixties—left their car and started walking toward Gatlinburg, which they hopefully thought was "just around the corner."

At 3:00 A.M. the next morning Ennis Ownby and John Dallard Ownby, who were operating a park snowplow found the two women, who had walked seven and a half miles from where they left their car. Mrs. Cuniff was dead and Dr. Spink was suffering severely from exposure. The survivor was taken to a Gatlinburg physician then to a Sevierville hospital, and the body of Mrs. Cuniff was taken to a Sevierville mortuary.

This experience recalls Whittier's oft-quoted lines: "For of all the sad words of tongue or pen . . ." The snow-bound women had walked seven and a half miles in the wrong direction. Had they walked back only four miles in the other direction it would have taken them to a home in the upper edge of Townsend where they could have gotten the needed help.

🍂   🍂   🍂

Although there are no records of hoarfrost frequency, in 1947 we did start keeping snowfall records for a period of eight years. The chief fact conveyed by these records is that there is *no* regularity to the snows, either as to the frequency or total amounts of snow. It snows more, and more often, at Clingmans Dome than at Newfound Gap. But records from Clingmans Dome are not so easily available because the road is closed during winter months. For this reason, the measurements from Newfound Gap have been used in the snowfall studies. Records at this 5,045-foot gap have been kept since 1939.

The question as to when, or how much, it will snow can not be answered. Surprising extremes are found in close proximity. There were only 4 inches—a total of 4 inches, if you please—for the full period of twelve consecutive months from February 1, 1946, through January 31, 1947—at Newfound Gap! At the other extreme, there was a total of 48.5 inches the very next month, the short month of February 1947!

The winter of 1939–40 saw a total snowfall of 120 inches at Newfound Gap. The following winter had only 77 inches, and, surprisingly, all of that 77 inches fell during the months of February and March of 1941. The average yearly snowfall for an eight-year period was 71 inches, with most of the big snows falling in February and March.

Rainfall is much more consistent. And one doesn't have to study the records to learn that it really does rain, and often, in the Smokies. Hikers learned long ago that it is necessary to be prepared for rain when going into the Smokies. It is significant that many hikers refer to Mt. LeConte as "Leaky." Records merely give the drippy details.

My first analysis of TVA's rainfall data for the Great Smokies was made in 1938, when I checked the 1936 and 1937 rainfall figures. That analysis showed that, during those two years, there were exactly 365 days with some rain. That, of course, is rain on an average of every other day. The showers were not that regular, of course. Occasionally it would rain as many as ten or twelve days in a row. At other times there were as many consecutive days with no rain.

A check of rainfall records for later years shows a slight change downward from the 1936–37 totals and frequency. The automatically reported rainfall at Clingmans Dome for the two earlier years averaged 88 inches per year. The total for 1946 was 84.98 inches. The twelve-year average for this mountaintop point is 81.63 inches. The average yearly rainfall for Gatlinburg is 51.48 inches, while at the Knoxville airport it is 47.39 inches.

The 1946 rain frequency at Clingmans Dome was 174 days *with* rain as opposed to 191 *without;* for Gatlinburg there were 122 days with rain and 243 without; and for Knoxville 120 with rain and 245 without.

The frequency of rains in the mountains, as well as the high total rainfall, contributes to the lush vegetation growth of the Smokies. Dense plant growth covers almost every boulder or fallen tree, as well as the ground itself. It is not unusual to see shrubs and trees as many as two or three inches in diameter growing atop horizontal branches of other tree species. Shrubs and wildflowers may be seen growing from tiny crevices high up the walls of sheer cliffs.

These rains also feed some exceptionally beautiful mountain streams, punctuated here and there by lacy waterfalls and picturesque cascades. It has been rumored, too, that some of these streams are inhabited by trout, bass, and other fish.

☞   ☞   ☞

Now, let us turn to another phase of mountain weather for which we have information, that of temperatures. The records that I have used in this study are from the automatically recording hygrothermographs at Newfound Gap and Gatlinburg, and from records for Knoxville furnished by the U.S. Weather Bureau, located at the airport.

It is well to remember that at the time the study was made, we had temperature records from the top of the Smokies for only one year. We must recognize the fact that figures for such a short period can not be very significant, but they do give a general idea of the situation. Here is some information based on the analysis of this one-year record.

Elevation is a major influence, especially on daytime or maximum temperatures. Daily *minimum* readings, however, are also influenced by a number of other factors such as wind, air drainage, and radiation. This report, however, is not so much concerned with the causes of the weather as with the weather itself. I have simply endeavored to present those bits of information that have been most interesting to me and which I believe will be of interest to other laymen in the field of mountain weather. The causes of weather, although often interesting in themselves, can be extremely complicated.

Regardless of the cause or causes, it is interesting to know that the temperature at Newfound Gap, on the crest of the Smokies, is often warmer than that at Gatlinburg, at the base of the mountains. It may be just as appropriate to say that it is often colder at Gatlinburg than at the gap. This is especially true with daily *minimum* temperatures. Also, it is occasionally warmer at Newfound Gap than at Knoxville.

In the day-to-day differentials, however, is where we find the real vagaries of temperatures. On twenty-two days of 1946 the daily minimum temperature at Newfound Gap was as warm as, or warmer than, at Knoxville. If that is not unexpected enough, note this: on exactly one hundred days of that one year the daily *minimum* temperature was as warm, or warmer, at the gap than at Gatlinburg. It is even more amazing to know that on eighty-three of those one hundred days it was actually warmer, instead of colder, at Newfound Gap, whereas the other seventeen days had the same temperature at both points.

As was to be expected, most of the temperature inversions occurred in the daily *minimums* rather than in the daily maximums. Also, most of them were in autumn and winter.

Cool, or moderately cold, weather provides some of the best hiking opportunities. One can be more comfortable while hiking even on a cold day than on most summer days. Another compensation for winter hiking lies in the fact that many fine views are provided after winter's defoliation of the deciduous trees. During the summer months the heavy foliage would screen out many of these views.

It does get hot, too, in the Smokies, although not often. The highest temperature at Newfound Gap in 1946 was eighty-three degrees and that only once. The high for Gatlinburg was ninety-one, while for Knoxville it was ninety-four. Only on nine days did the temperature at Newfound Gap register as high as eighty degrees, as compared with 111 days at Gatlinburg and 128 days at Knoxville with eighty degrees or hotter. As already indicated, it never rose to ninety degrees at the gap, whereas Gatlinburg had 9 and Knoxville 31 such days.

Do not get the impression, however, that it is always hot, or even warm, during the summer in the mountains. Such is not the case, as any hiker and many a motorist can testify. I have been uncomfortably cool, even in bright midday sun, almost every month of the summer. Although the year 1946 had no extremes in this respect, a study of the daily maximums will show several days that were in the comfortable to cool range of temperatures.

But when it is warm or even hot during the day, the late afternoon and night temperatures are usually comfortably cool—and sometimes just plain cold—in the higher elevations. The same is true to a slightly less extent at Gatlinburg. As already reported, the Gatlinburg temperatures, especially at night, are frequently cooler than those at Newfound Gap.

The *lowest* temperatures for the summer of 1946—June 1 through September 22—are Newfound Gap, thirty-five degrees; Gatlinburg, thirty-nine degrees; Knoxville, forty-six degrees. These were, of course, in the daily minimums. The lowest of the daily maximum temperatures at Newfound Gap was fifty-seven degrees, as compared with sixty-eight degrees for Gatlinburg and sixty-nine degrees for Knoxville.

So when planning a trip to the Great Smokies, one should not pay too much attention to the existing weather in Knoxville. And it is seldom advisable to change plans when hiking or motoring in the Smokies. The three following illustrations are of interest.

Dr. Eben Alexander Jr. (who then was a medical student), West Barber, Guy Frizzell, and I had planned an overnight hike to Mt. LeConte. The night was to be spent at the spot then known as Grass Patch, which is now designated as the Alum Cave Bluff Parking Area because it is the starting point for the Alum Cave Bluff Trail. On the starting day the clouds were hanging low over Knoxville, but about an hour before starting time they opened up with a terrific downpour that continued for at least thirty minutes after we started driving toward our camping site. That, of course, was before there were any park regulations on camping, because now it is not permitted at that spot.

By the time we reached Sevierville, we found that it had not even rained there; we had a perfectly dry camp that night and a delightful hike the next day.

A few years later Mrs. Campbell and I were taking two friends, Mr. and Mrs. W. K. Nuckolls, on a motor trip to the end of Clingmans Dome Road, planning to make the half-mile hike up the beaten path to the old wooden tower on Clingmans Dome. That, by the way, was the second wooden tower I had seen and used atop Clingmans Dome.

When we reached Newfound Gap, the clouds were down on the mountain and so dense that, as we stood at the Rockefeller Memorial, we could not see the bank and trees at the opposite side of the gap. All three of my companions felt that we should turn back, that there was no point in driving farther in clouds so heavy that it was actually difficult to see the edge of the road. Having had more experience with such situations, I used all the optimism I could command and told them that we might actually get above that blanket of clouds if we went on out to the end of Clingmans Dome Road. It was with much reluctance that they agreed, but we did go on with the original plans. Even to my surprise, we came out above the clouds just before we reached Indian Gap, and from there on we were looking down on solid banks of fleecy white clouds, with clear and deep blue skies overhead.

At the end of the road our wives decided that they would remain in the car instead of hiking up through the balsam (fir) forest to the tower, so Mr. Nuckolls and I went on without them. As we reached the observation platform at the top of the tower, the sight that spread out before us was breathtaking in its beauty and grandeur. The top of the clouds were from five thousand to fifty-five hundred feet above sea level, and so dense that it resembled a turbulent ocean with islands rising above it here and there. We could see all of Mt. LeConte except Balsam Point, at the extreme west end. To the right we could see Mt. Mingus and Mt. Kephart.

Such a sight is truly indescribable. Mr. Nuckolls and I were determined that our wives should also see it, so we went down to the car and finally were able to persuade them to go back with us. The four of us stayed on the tower for quite a long time; it was such an unusual sight that it was difficult to leave it.

On another occasion during a winter hike to Mt. LeConte, with about six inches of snow on the ground, my group met two young men coming down the trail. The point at which we met was less than half of a mile from LeConte Lodge. When we asked about the visibility on top, we were surprised to learn that they had just turned back, and therefore had not gotten

View from an observation tower at Clingmans Dome.

any of the rewards for such a difficult climb. It was their first trip up LeConte, and they had no way of knowing how much farther it was to the top—and for fear that it was a much greater distance, they had abandoned the climb in despair.

When we told them that we were within a very short distance, they joined our party and went on to the top. It was a particularly clear day, and the views were breathtaking. Thus, with just a very small amount of additional effort, they had a glorious experience that they had been about to miss.

Most mountain rains that I have experienced were on the gentle side, often lasting for hours. But at least a few times each year we had an old-fashioned "gully washer," as the foothills farmers called them, or, what was to us, a cloudburst. In the summer of 1927, just after we had watched a beautiful sunrise from Myrtle Point of Mt. LeConte, we could see that a hard rain was approaching from the west. Most of us hurried back to the shelter of the original LeConte Lodge before the storm struck. Brockway Crouch, however, went to Cliff Top to watch the approaching storm. Just as he reached that vantage point, he said that the storm struck with great fury, and when the rain hit him, it was as though someone had thrown a bucket of water upward into his face. What happened, of course, was that, as the first raindrops fell, they were swept back upward by the strong air currents that came up the precipitous face of Cliff Top. This process was repeated until the wind could hold the water no longer, and it was dumped very suddenly on the mountain, but being swept in a horizontal or slightly upward direction by the strong wind.

Although the intensity of the storm diminished somewhat after an hour or so, it kept raining very hard for several hours. Rather than face such a cloudburst, we lingered for a few hours longer than we had planned. That, of course, was before the days of graded trails on LeConte, and the beaten path had the appearance of a sizable stream. Then, when we reached points where the "trail" crossed the headwaters of LeConte Creek, that stream, usually a tiny thing, was so deep it was difficult to cross.

As we approached the top of Rainbow Falls, there was much concern about the ability of some of the inexperienced hikers to cross safely. The creek, normally about two or three feet wide and four to six inches deep at this point, was now at least fifteen feet wide and five or six feet deep. It would have been almost suicidal to attempt the usual crossing at the top of the falls—just about ten feet from where the stream started the downward plunge. It was agreed that every member of the party must cross on a fallen tree that was about a foot in diameter and eight or ten feet above the swirling water. Alex Harris and I were afraid that someone might fall off that hazardous "foot log" even though most of them were crawling rather than walking. Since we did not want to frighten them any more than they were already, we said nothing. Instead, we went downstream until we found a small but strong tree close to the edge of the stream—with the idea that if someone should take an unexpected tumble one of us could hold to the tree and anchor the other until he could reach and rescue the person who had fallen in. Although we were much relieved when every member had made the crossing safely, we then had to go back and crawl across the log ourselves, realizing that, should we slip off, there would be no one down there to catch us.

Never before had we seen Rainbow Falls as such a spectacular sight. Practically every bit of the water was hitting twenty-five to fifty feet farther downstream than usual. It was not falling straight down, as we usually saw it, but was plunging out and down, thus producing a thrilling spectacle. Pictures made that day by photographer Jim Thompson were still widely used as late as 1967.

Another cloudburst even more pronounced in its fury and in the amount of damage struck Mt. LeConte and vicinity on Labor Day, September 1, 1951. At LeConte Lodge, which is near the summit on the north slope, the rain gauge showed that a total of four inches of rain had fallen within the short space of one hour, with lighter rain still falling after that one-hour period. There was little or no damage done to trails or otherwise on the north side of the mountain. The real deluge hit near the top of the south slope. There was so much water falling in a very short time that several large landslides resulted. Large trees were swept down along with uncountable tons of earth and stone, creating some huge logjams near the foot of the mountain. Some of these caused Alum Cave Creek to change its course several feet to one side or the other. The water of Styx Branch, which flows through rugged and picturesque Huggins Hell, was a dark reddish brown for many months as a result of iron pigments that were uncovered in the slides that started near Myrtle Point.

Landslides wiped out short sections of the Alum Cave Bluffs trail in two spots—one about a mile below the Bluffs and the other about the same distance above the Bluffs. The upper slide left a very steep slope of solid rock, with no trace of the former trail remaining.

A trailside sign was erected by the interpretive branch of the Park Service, giving condensed information about the severity of that cloudburst so that later visitors using the trail could better understand some of the things they were seeing along the trail.

Far greater damage was done to the Newfound Gap Highway (U.S. 441). It was completely washed out in a few spots and rendered impassable until park road crews could provide temporary detours. An automobile was stranded for three or four hours between two of the washouts. The cost of rebuilding and repairing the road was more than two hundred thousand dollars.

Much damage was done in Gatlinburg also. A number of buildings were flooded, but the most spectacular damage there was that two cars were washed from their parking spaces in front of Greystone Hotel and wrecked as they were swept down with the turbulent waters of the river.

Although the storm was centered on Mt. LeConte, particularly on the south slope, the surrounding area also felt part of its fury; Elkmont, across Sugarland Mountain from Gatlinburg, saw a very sudden rise in the east prong of Little River. Loye W. Miller, then editor of the *Knoxville News-Sentinel,* was swimming with friends in the pool of the Appalachian Club. He told about hearing a big roar coming from upstream. When he looked for the source of the noise, he saw a high wall of water rushing toward him. Most of the other members of the swimming party barely reached safety on the high bank of the river, but Loye climbed a nearby small tree from which he watched the spectacle of the swirling and tumbling water as it rushed past.

In the early park days there were very few foot logs to help us cross the streams more safely. When we were returning from a rainy trip, with the streams somewhat swollen, it was difficult, and sometimes a bit dangerous, to cross by rock hopping. On many trips we men who were wearing water-proofed, high-topped boots stood in water that was a foot or more deep to offer a steadying hand to those who were jumping from one boulder to another in the middle of a stream. This possibly prevented a number from slipping into the swollen stream.

Mountain streams can, and sometimes do, rise with frightening swiftness following a rain of cloudburst proportions. Such rains may have been limited to a headwater's location, with very little or no rain at a downstream location where park visitors were swimming or otherwise enjoying the water. A terrible incident of this nature occurred on August 7, 1947, when a flash flood sent a high wall of water rushing down the West Prong of Little Pigeon River, causing the death of Miss Rose Mary Mathias, a twenty-three-year-old woman from Frostburg, Maryland.

Miss Mathias and three other young women were sunbathing on a mid-stream rock near the confluence of Alum Cave and Road Prongs of the river, only an hour or so after their arrival at Gatlinburg. Two of the young women saw the floodwaters approaching and rushed to the safety of the stream bank. A third member of the party, twenty-three-year-old Miss Madeline Stokum, of New York, was caught in the floodwaters, but managed to escape by hanging onto shrubs at the side of the stream. She received several cuts and bruises on her legs, and suffered from exposure and shock. Miss Mathias, however, was not so fortunate, as she was caught in the flood and swept off the rock and carried downstream by the mad rush of the high water. A vigorous search for her body extended late into the night, and was started again at daybreak the next morning. It was found about two hundred yards above the Chimneys Campground, which is more than a mile downstream from where she had been sunbathing.

Another drowning tragedy occurred on October 6, 1950, when George Michon, a twenty-three-year-old bridegroom from Yonkers, New York, stepped on a wet rock and slipped into the swirling water immediately below the rapids at the Sinks on Little River. The horrified bride, who was a good swimmer, made frantic but unsuccessful efforts to rescue her honeymooning husband, who could not swim. She had the agonizing experience of seeing him swept out of sight and to a drowning death by the treacherous undercurrents.

Park officials warn all users of mountain streams always to be on the alert to the many dangers of these streams. Swimmers, sunbathers, picnickers, or fishermen should familiarize themselves with the immediately surrounding topography so they know the best escape route for use in the event of suddenly approaching high water. It is almost unbelievable how quickly a peaceful-looking mountain stream can become an instrument of sudden death.

Such violence does not occur very often, however. Usually it is from a few to several years from one incident to the next, but there is no predicting when a flash flood is to strike—and little or no warning when it does. Thus, it behooves all users of mountain streams to be alert at all times.

Hard and prolonged rains can become a major factor on almost any hike, especially when swollen streams are to be crossed without the aid of foot logs. Even so, most hikes have been completed as planned despite the added hardships and some danger caused by high water.

I recall a very few hikes where there was a change in destination, but I do not recall a single case where the hike was abandoned because of high water. Herbert Webster, however, does recall one case where the trip—wisely, as it turned out—was called off. It was a hike from Tapoco, North Carolina, to Little Fodderstack.

It had rained most of the morning of the first day, and was still raining when they stopped at a small clearing to make camp for the night. Only a few of the hikers had adequate rain gear, and Herbert was not one of the lucky ones. He just pulled a hood down over his head and tried to imagine that he was keeping dry.

Herbert recalls that Wiley Oakley, the famed mountain guide from Gatlinburg, was in the party, and that he regaled the rain-soaked campers with some of his tall tales, one of which told about his gun with a crooked barrel "for shooting around trees."

Early the next morning the rain was still falling, so much so that some of the hikers just decided to skip breakfast rather than try to cook in the rain. The hike leaders explored the trail for a short distance but turned back when they encountered a creek that was far out of its banks. As they returned, they announced that the hike was being called off.

When they again reached Tapoco, they found the river there to be an awesome thing. But Herbert tells that their embarrassment because of having to give up the hike was tempered considerably by later news that the river at Tapoco had continued to rise and a short time later had become completely impassable.

Herbert said that pictures of the dejected campers made that morning before they turned back were described as looking more like photographs of a group of war refugees.

Sudden and severe drops in temperature are experienced occasionally in the Great Smokies, as twenty-five Knoxville hikers and fifty visiting scientists, whom I had recruited for a mid-winter trip to Mt. LeConte, can attest. It was the last day of 1927, and it was a relatively mild day, but with drizzling rain, as the group left Knoxville. Insofar as we knew, there was no indication of impending extreme weather, but by the time we were ready to start the hike from Cherokee Orchard, it was noticeably colder, so much so that most of the drivers drained their radiators. (Antifreeze preparations were not in general use in those days.) Even so, Brockway Crouch's thermometer registered a mild forty degrees, and a little snow was falling.

Many of the scientists were not experienced hikers, and the progress was rather slow. Due to the difference in elevation and to the fact that a nationwide blizzard had struck, the temperature had dropped almost to the zero mark by the time we reached LeConte Lodge.

The lodge then in use was a chinked log structure with a sloping dirt floor and with the wood-burning fireplace at the upper end. The "beds" consisted of thick layers of balsam (Fraser fir) branches on double-deck supports on both sides of a wide center aisle. Since the huge fireplace was six or eight feet higher than the door at the lower end of the lodge, and since heat rises perceptibly, almost none of the warmth reached the lower end of the building. We knew, therefore, that we were in for a very cold night, and we carried in all of the firewood that could be stacked in the space provided. Big sticks of wood were added as soon as those that were already on the fire had burned down enough to make room for another one.

It became abundantly clear to the shivering hikers that "the bottom was about to drop out of the thermometer." Although the fire was kept going full blast, the temperature became so low that those who had retired soon learned that they could not keep warm, even with their woolen blankets wrapped about them, and they again rejoined those who were still trying to stay close enough to the fire to keep from freezing.

The informal seating and standing arrangements called for a few to sit on the floor between the long bench and the fire. The next group crowded as close together as possible on the bench, the center of which was only about five or six feet from the fireplace. Others, necessarily on their feet, kept milling about. Those who were on the floor were soon so hot that they retreated to the rear, as others took their places. The result was that most of the hikers were uncomfortably cold as others were equally uncomfortable from the intense heat that, unfortunately, never reached very far back into the lodge. This called for a constant changing of places throughout the night. Only a very few, however, found it desirable to face the raw cold outside the lodge, even for a few minutes.

The drinking water at LeConte Lodge in those early days was kept in a big bucket, with a dipper from which to get a drink. Brockway Crouch, who was seated at the end of the bench, not more than ten feet from the fully stoked fireplace, became thirsty and reached for a dipper of water, which he could do without having to get up from his seat. To his great surprise, he lifted the entire bucket of water, which had become a solid block of ice, and he had to do without the drink that he wanted.

It was too cold to sleep, and much too cold to take a walk. The "imprisoned" hikers passed the time in a variety of ways, with group singing possibly consuming most of the time. Storytelling was another popular diversion. With two British scientists in the group, most of the others recalled and told a great variety of stories in which an Englishman was the butt of the joke. Even the visiting Britishers told a few on themselves.

Dr. L. R. Hesler, then head of the University of Tennessee Department of Botany and later dean of the College of Liberal Arts, proved himself to be quite adept at writing limericks. With lots of "help" from others, he produced a total of fourteen jingles, most of them about some member of the group. No one bothered to do any editing, and none of the productions could be classed as "literature."

The most amazing "entertainment" during that cold night was the card tricks performed by a General Electric engineer named Gluesing, whose first name has been misplaced and forgotten. Despite the fact that magicians are said to prefer performing their stunts at, or slightly above, eye level, Mr. Gluesing worked very effectively with a crowd standing all around him and looking down on every move he made. Even so, he kept us guessing as the numerous tricks unfolded before our very eyes. He told us that he had financed his college education by performing his card stunts before civic clubs and other groups.

Mr. Gluesing told us, and insisted that it was true, that he actually liked the kind of severe winter that we were then experiencing. By way of proving his point, he made a few trips out into the bitter cold and remained long enough to do a few handsprings, for which he had very few onlookers.

Each member of the Knoxville group had been assigned the task of caring for the needs of two visitors. One of the scientists, who was under the care of Brockway Crouch, was a man from Florida. He, perhaps, was less prepared for such temperatures than were most of the others.

The temperature had dropped to twenty degrees *below zero* early the next morning, the first day of 1928, as we prepared to brave the elements in an effort to see the sunrise from Myrtle Point, almost a mile from LeConte Lodge. Within a few minutes the Florida visitor was wearing more and more of Brockway's winter clothing, including his hat with fleece-lined earflaps. Brockway experienced a frostbitten ear, but, thanks to a later application of a salve normally used in the treatment of burns, there were no serious consequences.

As we returned to our cars at Cherokee Orchard, after an icy descent, most of us were able to get our cars started, after having refilled our radiators. Not so for Jim Thompson, then president of the hiking club. His car

End of Skyway (center) and Andrews Bald as seen from the trail to Clingmans Dome, November 20, 1937.

had suffered a cracked engine block, which made it necessary for him to have his car pulled back to Knoxville. Jim still insists that one can not know the full discomfort of subzero temperature until he sits alone in the seat of a car in which the motor is not running, while guiding the car as it is being pulled back home.

This is one trip in which it took a few weeks in retrospect before we could experience very much enjoyment from the outing.

Other details of this unusual trip may be found on pages 42 and 43 of *Birth of a National Park,* published in 1960 by the University of Tennessee Press, and of which I am the author.

Here are a few selections from the limericks written atop Mt. LeConte on that cold, cold winter night.

This one is about "Red" Camp, then a botany professor at Ohio State University:

"A fellow from Ohio named Camp
Hair as red as the light of a lamp
As quick as a flash
With his little mustache
The flappers in his class he would vamp."

Our cold weather engineer-magician was kidded with the following bits of alleged humor:

"There was a magician named Gluesing
Who's so slick 'twould appear he'd been greasing,
With cards and a thimble
He's really quite nimble
His friends he always was fleecing."

Dr. Cy Crosby, a spider authority from Cornell who had done quite a bit of research in the Smokies, and who was a member of the party, drew the following lines:

"There was a bug man named Cy
On the mountains he always was spry,
He hunted a spider
But he drank too much cider
And now we fear he will die!"

Charles I. Barber, a leading architect who had designed several of the then-new buildings for the University of Tennessee, came in for this tribute:

"Barber is the name of a man who is tall,
Among architects he is best of them all,
Buildings he would design
For the university so fine
We know that they never will fall."

Dr. Hesler, leader of the limerick writing, was the object of the following "literary gem:"

"There was a young man from Cornell
The names of most plants he could tell
His first name was Lex,
Hunted spores with his specks,
And now he's in Huggins Hell."

Even I was the object of one of the ditties, and it is obvious that they were kinder to me than to some of the others.

"There was a nice man named Campbell
Up the mountain trails he would scramble
Nothing more would he want
Than a trip up LeConte.
Oh Lord! How that bird does ramble."

Copies of the fourteen limericks were sent to members of the party as souvenirs of that cold night near the top of Mt. LeConte.

For many of the visiting scientists it was their first hike in the Great Smokies. Despite the extreme discomfort experienced on that trip, many of them returned to see these rugged mountains under more pleasant conditions.

A drizzling rain was encountered on a hiking club trip from Cades Cove to Thunderhead. Because of the rain, the hikers planned to eat lunch in the abandoned herders' cabin near the west end of Spence Field. But the first few to enter the cabin came out rather hurriedly when they learned that they had already gotten covered with hungry fleas that had infested the cabin. This cabin, which was on the North Carolina side about fifty yards from the crest, or state line, was the last in a succession of five cabins that provided shelter for Cades Cove herders.

Since the lunches then had to be eaten in the rain, most of the hikers started back down the Bote Mountain trail as soon as they could, thus passing up the plan to hike eastward about two miles along the main crest to the high point of Thunderhead. Five of us, however, decided that we would complete the trip as planned, regardless of the weather, which we did. My companions on this rainy extra hiking were A. G. "Dutch" Roth, Ralph Crisco, Willa Love Galyon, and Bess Avery. We agreed that it would be easier and quicker if we left our packs in the trail that started down Bote Mountain. While we were on the higher points of Thunderhead, it not only kept raining, but the clouds descended upon us. They became so dense that one could not see other members of the small group as much as fifteen or twenty feet away.

As a result of the lost visibility we passed all the way through Spence Field, but didn't know it until we reached the forest at the west end of the mountaintop meadow. Realizing that we had gone too far, we retraced our steps and began hunting for our packs. When we failed to find them as we kept close together, we spread out a bit—talking back and forth to be sure that we were staying together. That didn't help; we still couldn't find the packs.

Remembering that the place where we had left them was on the Tennessee side of the meadow, directly across from the herders' cabin, I told the others that we surely could find the cabin, and then we would be more likely to find the packs by just crossing the meadow. I volunteered to undertake that task, insisting that my companions keep talking so I at least would be able to find them even though I could not see them.

I then started out in the direction that I, and all of the others, knew to be southward—since that was the direction of the cabin. To my amazement I ran directly into our packs—proving that I had gone in exactly the opposite direction from what we had thought. Although we still couldn't see each other, they all heard my rejoicing and joined me, after which we headed on down the mountain. I wouldn't have believed it had someone told me that five persons could all get so completely turned around when walking through a sea of clouds that were so thick that one could almost slice them. But now we know it.

✐   ✐   ✐

As is implied by its very name Thunderhead, this 5,530-foot peak on the state line and overlooking picturesque Cades Cove often has thunderheads of cumulus clouds hanging over it. Although in most cases they float beautifully a thousand feet or more above the crest, another trip is recalled in which we were enveloped in clouds almost as dense as on the trip just described. I went along with a park maintenance crew, which was working under the supervision of Charles S. Dunn, then chief ranger for the park. My task was to point out to them the exact route of the Appalachian Trail from Clingmans Dome to Spence Field. They were to mark the trail and do a little preliminary clearing. The hiking club is not permitted to do any clearing within the park, even on the AT.

With horses to carry the camping equipment, trail-clearing tools, and food, we made good progress and had a delightful three days in the high Smokies. But when we reached cloud-shrouded Thunderhead, it was next to impossible to see which of the many "paths" the Appalachian Trail was to follow. Grazing cattle had made a maze of "trails." In clear weather one can easily see which path the AT follows, but as already mentioned, what we encountered was something less than clear weather. For that reason, we had to postpone the trail marking for the two miles across the several "tops" of Thunderhead to Spence Field until more suitable weather. Incidentally, trail marking across these mountaintop meadows is done best by building stone cairns beside the trail—and they must be high enough to be seen in deep snow.

As we moved slowly along the downhill crest of Thunderhead, I made a picture of one of the packhorses from about fifteen feet. Although my exposure was correct, the clouds were so dense that it was difficult to see the horse in that picture.

It was also the network of cattle paths that made it so hard to find our hiking packs on the previous trip. Although we thought we were following one that led down to the beginning of the Bote Mountain Trail, we had accidentally taken one that continued along the crest—until we ran into the forest at the west end of Spence Field.

On another hike we were walking through clouds that were so dense that we could not see others of the group who were as much as ten or fifteen feet away. It was, of course, difficult to stay on the beaten path that served as a trail. After a half mile or so, in which we could not see any of the nearby landmarks, some of us had difficulty in knowing just where we were at the moment. The man in front came to a familiar point and said, "Oh, now I know where we are."

"Yes, but we don't know where you are" was the remark made by Ernest Fryar, one of the hikers at the rear of the group.

The moral to be seen in these experiences is that extreme care must be taken when hiking in thick clouds where there is no graded trail. It doesn't take but a few minutes to become completely turned around, as we learned on the earlier trip.

The reference here to both fog and clouds recalls the answer of the meteorologist who was then in charge of the U.S. Weather Bureau in Knoxville. I asked him to tell me the difference between clouds and fog. At first he told me that, by general usage, it is fog if it touches the ground—and a cloud if it is up in the air. When one who is in the valley or foothills sees the fluffy white stuff resting on a mountaintop, it is a cloud to him—but the hiker who is in it is just as likely to use one name as the other. This weatherman friend then added, "Both clouds and fog are man-made names for the same natural phenomenon—condensed moisture."

"Winds blow almost constantly in the Smokies." Because most of the time it is just a gentle breeze, hikers may be inclined to contradict this statement that wildflower photographers (and there are many of them along the roads and trails) know to be a fact. I have seen Dr. William F. Hutson, who made most of the exquisite pictures in *Great Smoky Mountains Wildflowers,* and Jim Thompson, veteran photographer, as well as others, wait—as patiently as possible—for many minutes before the flower would be still enough to have its picture taken.

At times, however, we have very strong gales, especially on the wind-swept mountaintops. Once while camped in Spence Field, near Thunder-head, we had to fasten our tents down more securely. And when we started to walk, we had to lean into the wind to prevent being blown off balance. These steady winds, however, seldom do much damage, if any.

Throughout the park we can see grim evidence that winds of a different type have struck. Although twisters or tornadoes usually reach their maxi-mum strength or velocity high above the ground, they do touch down at widely separated spots, snapping trees off as though they were toothpicks. In such cases most of the trees are broken off just a few feet above the ground, but some are broken off many feet higher. The areas in which the virgin forest trees have been leveled off are very small, just an acre or so in most cases.

Certain species of wildflowers "move in" soon after a blow-down has occurred. These are flowers that like the climate and soil of the high Smokies, but require more light than they get in heavily forested areas. The lovely monkshood (*Aconitum uncinatum*) is such a flower. Then the slow but steady process of reforestation gets underway, requiring several decades before the permanent forest is reestablished.

Two blow-downs that occurred in the first half of the twentieth century and which have been seen by great numbers of hikers include one that is next to the upper end of Andrews Bald and near Clingmans Dome and another that is on Mt. LeConte, just a few hundred yards or so west of LeConte Lodge. Gene Gooch, Jr., and a small group of friends were spend-ing the night in the old balsam-bough beds of the original lodge when the tornado hit very close to them. They were awakened by the loud rattling of the pots and pans that were suspended under the nearby shedlike roof that served as an open-air kitchen. Gene recalls that no actual damage was done to the lodge or the "kitchen," but that the roar of the tornadic winds and the continuous rattling of the kitchen utensils kept them awake most of the night. Even with all that commotion during the night, they were not prepared for what they saw as they were leaving the lodge the next morning. Mature spruce and fir (balsam) trees, some of them almost three feet in diameter, had been snapped off or uprooted, and left piled in a tangled mass that was almost impenetrable. Other trees just a few feet away had not been disturbed.

This blow-down provided Jack Huff with a convenient source of firewood for use at his lodge. By the time these tree trunks had been removed, blackberry plants had made a thick ground cover. Two quarts of large juicy blackberries picked from this blow-down in 1935 provided the dessert at the evening meal for my father and other relatives who had climbed LeConte with me. Incidentally, the species of blackberry that grows at such Great Smokies elevations does not have the thorns that torment berry pickers in the valleys around the foothills of the Smokies.

While on overnight hikes the conversations around the campfires often turned to freakish or unusual weather that various hikers had experienced. On such occasions the late Dr. H. M. Jennison, University of Tennessee botanist and hiking club president, frequently delighted us as he told about the strong winds of his native Montana.

"Out there the wind really blew," he would start. "It was so strong that the orthodox weather bureau instruments wouldn't last an hour," he would add as he warmed up to his subject. "Our wind gauges were heavy chains suspended from the top of a strong post. In such winds as we have here in the Smokies, the chain would just swing slowly back and forth. To us that was just a lull between real winds. We paid no attention until it began to swing out almost horizontally and even that was just a normal wind. We never became really excited until the links began snapping off from the end of the chain. That is when we started for the storm cellars," he would conclude.

WILDLIFE

BEARS

Bears were very scarce in the Great Smokies when the national park was being established. The few that had survived the ruthless hunting methods, and the numerous forest fires that followed in the wake of timber cutting, were extremely shy and were seldom seen by hikers. They had learned that man was their most deadly enemy, and when they saw, heard, or smelled a person, they immediately ran for the protective cover of the surrounding trees and shrubs. I had hiked rather intensively throughout various sections of the Smokies about fifteen years before I saw my first wild bear.

The lead story in the August 1934 issue of the *American Rifleman* was my article with the title "The Great Smokies: A Big Game Preserve." In that story I told of the existing situation with reference to bears. Further, I predicted that the protection then being given to all forms of wildlife would enable the bruins to increase in number to the point that they would expand their range into surrounding forest lands on which bear hunting was permitted during specified open seasons.

The principal character in my *American Rifleman* story was "Uncle" George Whaley who was then seventy-five years old. He had lived in the beautiful Greenbrier section, approximately ten miles east of Gatlinburg and at the foot of majestic Mt. LeConte, until he sold his mountainous land to the park commission and moved several miles from the park border. He told me about his own bear hunting experiences and about the more extensive exploits of his father.

"I have seen bears come within twenty-five feet of our house and eat apples," Uncle George said. "For many years there were so many bears we couldn't raise hogs or cattle. We depended entirely upon bear meat and venison, and that was not hard to get. I saw my father kill five bears, a deer and a wild turkey gobbler in one day."

"When more than one bear or deer was killed on the same trip," he explained, "the animals were skinned and dressed, after which the carcasses were sunk in a cold mountain stream, and the skins taken home. The hunters would then go back for the meat, making as many trips as necessary."

"The cold water washed the blood out of the animals, and made the meat better," Uncle George said. "Meat for a whole year's supply was stored in the smokehouse—a specially built structure about ten or twelve feet square, which stood a few feet away from the cabin. Our smokehouse was always well filled with bear meat and venison."

"My father was a good hunter, and took good care of his rifle-gun. He often cut new rifles in the barrel. He changed it from a flintlock to a cap-and-ball gun. I went hunting with him almost as far back as I can remember. On the longer hunting trips we would take dried venison as our only food. When we sliced it real thin it was mighty good eating."

Uncle George recalled that his father had killed hundreds of bears, and many deer and turkeys, with this one rifle. Then Uncle George himself used it for years. The stock was now no longer intact, but the barrel was one of his treasured possessions.

The later use of traps and dogs—and hunting during the breeding season—are ascribed as the chief reasons for the recent scarcity of big game in the Great Smokies. "I never used a dog unless the bears got to bothering my hogs and cattle," said Uncle George. "When you turn dogs on bears, the bears just move out to some other place." He recalled one time when, as a boy, he heard the dogs set up a great commotion near his house. His father grabbed the old rifle, and hastened to the scene of the disturbance, to find the dogs attacking a huge black bear that was raiding the barnyard. The two dogs had seized the bear, one by each ear. Whereupon the elderly Whaley laid down the gun, drew his long-bladed hunting knife and sunk it into the bear's heart.

Uncle George was regarded as one of the best shots in his community. "When I was squirrel hunting, I wouldn't walk three feet to get a rest for my rifle-gun; and I seldom missed. I have shot the head off many a squirrel. I shot them through the head because the homemade bullet would tear the body all to pieces." The largest bear ever killed by Uncle George weighed about 400 pounds. It took two men to carry it home, and they could not carry it more than 200 yards before having to stop for rest. The usual size of the bears was about 250 or 300 pounds.

Uncle George hadn't been bear hunting in five years, because the game had become so scarce, but he believed that the establishment of the Great Smoky Mountains National Park would in time make game again plentiful in that region. This is one of the reasons why he cooperated in the establishment of this park, and he not only sold his own land for park purposes, at a reasonable price, but also encouraged his neighbors to do likewise.

Seventy-five-year-old "Uncle" George Whaley with his father's
one-hundred-year-old "rifle-gun" barrel on April 29, 1934. The
stock was no longer intact, but the barrel was one of his treasured possessions.

A black bear starts up the steep bank above the Newfound Gap Highway, July 9, 1939.

A black bear cub, four or five months old, licking honey from a rock near Elkmont, Tennessee, in the Great Smoky Mountains National Park on August 25, 1935

Speaking of neighbors, they were more than just neighbors to Uncle George. Of the hundred or so families that lived in Greenbrier Cove, more than half were Whaleys, while most of the others were related to Whaleys. Uncle George was one of eleven children, and is the father of ten children. He had more than fifty grandchildren.

When they sold their land to the park commission, most of these people bought better land, or land that is more easily cultivated, in some other section. Most of them stayed in the foothills near the park boundary. A few, however, accepted the offer (which was made to all) to remain on their land through a lifetime lease. It was to the homes of these former neighbors, back in the Greenbrier Cove, that Uncle George and I went in search of old rifles.

The rifle was the constant companion of the early settler. He was dependent upon it for protection and for food. It was even carried to church; and these pioneers became famous for their nail-driving marksmanship. It was in nearby mountain foothills that Daniel Boone and Davy Crockett won their fame as riflemen; and pioneer histories give glowing accounts of the uncanny marksmanship of the East Tennessee contingent in the Battle of Kings Mountain. Rifle shooting was a part of the education of every young East Tennessean in those days.

⁂

Today all of that has changed. Hunting is almost a lost art in the southern mountains, and not permitted in the Great Smokies. Only a very few expert riflemen are to be found there now, the rapidly decreasing supply of big game being the principal reason for the decline of interest in rifle shooting.

In addition to the somewhat general use of traps and dogs, destructive lumbering methods have made heavy inroads into the supply of game. Most of the lumbermen left slashings over the mountainsides, to be consumed by fire—which almost inevitably followed close upon the heels of the lumbermen. These fires, a few of which were inside the park area before it became a park, and many of which were in the surrounding mountains, killed or drove out much of the game.

Whatever the cause, big game was almost gone from the Great Smokies when the national park was established. Had not this last stronghold of virgin wilderness in eastern America been saved from the lumberman's ax, and thus kept for a perpetual and absolute game refuge, deer, already practically driven from the area, would possibly have been exterminated. The supply of bears, wild turkeys, and ruffed grouse would have been endangered. Elk, beaver, and the mountain lion had already been completely driven from the region.

The situation had attracted the attention of leading sportsmen and conservationists, and progress was made in the effort to prevent hunting out of season. Game preserves were being established in portions of the national forests and on a few large private estates. This was a good beginning, but a small one. And then, at last, came the establishment of the Great Smoky Mountains National Park. The preservation of this rugged and primitive area of 510,000 acres, on both sides of the high-flung mountains that form the boundary between Tennessee and North Carolina, did not just happen. It was the result of a hard ten-year fight under the inspired leadership of Col. David C. Chapman of Knoxville, a life member of the National Rifle Association. One of Colonel Chapman's right-hand men in this great movement was Gen. Frank Maloney, also of Knoxville, and who has long been a director of the NRA.

In the Great Smokies we have a wilderness area that is seventy-two miles long and from ten to twenty miles wide. Inside this wildlife haven hunting is not permitted. With this protection, these mountains within a few years will be again plentifully supplied with big game. The complete cessation of hunting in so large an area will permit native animals to multiply rapidly. It will also cause them to become relatively tame, so park visitors can get good close-up views of them. This in itself will be the chief reward for camera-hunters and many other visitors.

But to sportsmen there is another and very important side of the picture. Surrounding the Great Smoky Mountains National Park on all sides are other mountains that are in private ownership or in national forests. As game becomes more abundant in the park, it will overflow into the surrounding mountains.

That was the end of the article in the *American Rifleman*. It is interesting to note that bears again were numerous much earlier than had been expected or predicted.

When bears—ours are the black bears—finally began to learn that they were no longer being hunted, and especially when they found that park visitors were providing a new source of food, they soon lost their fear of man. Within another few years they actually became pests around the trail shelters, campgrounds, and picnic areas.

Despite the fact that warnings have been posted along the park roads, telling visitors not to feed the bears, a surprising number of people persist in feeding them—often as a means of keeping the bears around so they can get more pictures. This had led to a number of people being injured each year. Some visitors have been bitten when the bear resented the fact that he was no longer being fed. Others were slapped or scratched. One woman, running from the bear she had been feeding, was badly scratched as she was climbing into her car. She had a doctor bill—and in addition had to pay a twenty-five-dollar fine for violating the "no feeding" park regulation. She is not likely to feed the bears again.

Before the bears became such pests, and safety hazards, a visitor occasionally had the pleasure of watching some of their interesting antics. The late O. M. Schantz of Chicago heard what he thought to be a child crying as he was hiking down the trail below Ramsey Cascades. Upon investigation he saw a mother bear spanking one of her two cubs as she was forcing it to cross the stream. Mrs. Campbell and I saw another mother bear spanking a cub that she was trying to drive away from a garbage can. Although we were not feeding them, and had not been feeding them, we were eating some cookies as we sat in our car watching the cub get the spanking. Before we realized it the mother bear had left the cub and was heading straight to our car, evidently having smelled the cookies. Mrs. Campbell barely got the window raised as the mother bear's tongue was pressed against the glass of the car window. We learned, therefore, that it is dangerous to eat even in your car unless the windows are kept raised.

Shortly after we first began to see bears I learned that one was being seen regularly in a certain area near Elkmont. I wanted to get some bear pictures, and to lure it to a good picture-making spot I poured some syrup on a small boulder. Within a few minutes the bear appeared and soon found the syrup, which he licked up very quickly. As he looked up I snapped the best bear picture that it has been my good fortune to make. Although I made five or six shots while he was at that spot, only the one was really good. It was so good that it was published in the August 1936 issue of the *National Geographic* magazine.

Long after the bears had become so numerous along the road between Gatlinburg and the top of the Smokies they were still scarce along the trails in other sections of the park. An interesting experience was enjoyed as Dr. and Mrs. William F. Hutson and I started on a hike from the Cosby Campground to Low Gap and Mt. Cammerer. When we had walked only a few hundred yards Bill remembered that he had not locked his car, and went back to do so. As Anna Katherine and I continued walking slowly up the trail we heard a commotion in the woods to our right and soon saw a big bear walking a log across the creek below us. It got off the log and continued slowly toward us, stopping frequently to turn over rocks and pieces of wood in search of grubs or any other food. Anna Katherine was frightened and said that she didn't want the bear to come any closer to us. I assured her that when he saw us he would be more afraid of us than she was of him. This explanation sufficed for only a few minutes, though the bear still had not seen us, and she again told me—rather emphatically—that she didn't want it to come *any* closer.

Telling Anna Katherine to watch the bear very closely, I yelled a loud *"Boo!"*

Hearing this unexpected sound, and upon seeing us, the bear turned very quickly and ran down the mountain as fast as he could go. Bill, who in the meantime had started back up the trail, reported that he had never seen such a frightened bear.

About the same time as that of the previous incident, a friend told me that he had just met a young couple that were newcomers to Knoxville, Mr. and Mrs. Charles A. Wagner, and that they were much interested in making some hiking trips. He asked me where they should go. When I explained that I could not give really helpful information without first learning what type of hiking they preferred, it was arranged for them to come to my office for a discussion. Upon learning that they wanted some real hiking, not just a Sunday afternoon walk, I recommended a three day expedition starting from the Cosby Campground and using the Cosby Knob trail shelter as a base of operations.

After a night of camping, they left their supplies and surplus clothing in the trail shelter—which had been a common and satisfactory practice up to that time. But when they returned to the shelter that afternoon, following a pleasant hike to Mt. Cammerer, they found that a "visitor" had been there. Supplies had been scattered about, and Charles could not find one of the shoes from the extra pair that he had brought for use in case he got his first pair wet. Although he never did find the lost shoe, it is my guess that Charles and Klovia Wagner would not have missed that experience for twice the cost of a pair of shoes. They continued to explore the trails of the Smokies for several years, until he was fatally stricken with polio.

Because so many people were around most of the time, LeConte Lodge, near the summit of Mt. LeConte, was not bothered with bears until a few years after they had been causing trouble at so many other places. But finally they began to make regular visits there, especially to the garbage pit several yards below the kitchen. In a few more years they began to raid the building where food was stored. Their strong jaws enabled them to puncture cans of food, and something had to be done, and quickly, to protect the valuable food—all of which had been carried up on horseback. When a dog failed to provide the needed protection, the erection and operation of an electric fence did the job. Many interesting antics were observed before the bears finally learned to "respect" the electric fence.

Bears, especially the cubs and other small bears, often climb trees in search of food. Favorite species of tree are the black cherry and the fire cherry when the berries are ripe. The smaller cubs will go way out on small branches until it appears that they are likely to fall out when the branches are forced down by their weight. Mother bears, sometimes called sows, often spank their cubs to make them climb a tree, or to go back up the tree if they try to come down too soon, when the mothers think the cubs might be in danger.

Female bears start breeding when they are a bit less than two years old, after which they breed every other year. The cubs, which are born in mid-winter, stay with the mother through the next winter and until just before time for her to breed again, at which time she drives them away and won't permit them to return to her.

Usually a bear gives birth to twins, with occasionally just one; equally rare is triplets. But, in about 1935, a mother with four cubs was seen quite regularly along Clingmans Dome Road. Park naturalists report that there is some possibility that only two of the four actually belonged to her, the other two having been "adopted" by her when their mother was killed or died a natural death. Even so, they say that most likely all four were born to her at the same time.

Interested visitors soon applied the name "Sadie" to this mother bear. Hundreds of people made, or tried to make, pictures of these mischievous cubs and the mother. Sadie would tolerate just so much of this, and often made displays of open hostility. One day I was standing guard, with a big club in my hand, as Jim Thompson was making some pictures on a big view camera. With his head under the focusing cloth, Jim had difficulty judging the distance from him to Sadie and continued adjusting his camera some-what after Sadie had come too close for safety. In an effort to drive her back, I raised my club in what I thought to be a threatening position. Then, with-out leaving her tracks, she lunged her body forward several inches and let out a loud growl.

I forgot all about my responsibility of protecting Jim, dropped my club and jumped backward for my own safety. At that point Jim decided that he had made all the pictures of Sadie that he cared to make.

The great interest in bears on the part of park visitors creates traffic snarls within a few minutes after a bear appears on the roadside. Sometimes, espe-cially on those few occasions when all of the visitors observe the no-feeding regulations, the bear will soon walk back into the woods, and traffic begins its normal flow again. But when the bear or bears, especially when cubs are present, linger in the roadway or at the roadside, the park rangers have to drive them away to prevent further traffic congestion. Their favorite "weapon" for several years was a pick handle, with which the ranger would give the bear a light tap across the nose, and the bruins would then beat a hasty retreat. They soon learned to respect the ranger's uniform, and espe-cially that formidable pick handle.

Sadie had obviously observed that I was not wearing the ranger's uni-form, and that the club with which I was attempting to frighten her was not the familiar and feared pick handle.

On another occasion a large crowd of park visitors was watching a big bear as it walked back and forth around and among the people. A ranger who was passing by stopped long enough to warn them that bears are actu-ally wild animals, despite their usual peaceable attitudes, and told them to keep a safe distance away.

As the ranger departed, one of the men reached over and patted the bear on the back as he said, "I will pat him, no matter what the ranger says." That was one case in which I almost wished that the bear had taught the offender a valuable lesson.

DEER

A Virginia white tail deer, though gotten as a fawn and raised as a pet, is still a wild animal—and, as such, quite dangerous. I learned this fact the hard way.

While on a trip in northern Georgia a friend gave a six-month-old fawn to Aaron Bill Vines, and Bill brought it back to Knoxville with him. This was in 1930. Bill kept him as a pet for about five years, but it finally became impossible to keep him in any normal fence enclosure. The buck, using his antlers for the purpose, would tear holes in a fence that he could not jump and escape. On the neighborhood forays his favorite food was flowers, especially roses. This made the buck quite unpopular with his neighbors, so the "pet" was turned over to Andy Huff, owner-proprietor of Gatlinburg's Mountain View Hotel. Andy built a strong, high fence around a five-acre wooded lot just back of the hotel, where all went well for about two years—most of the time, that is.

During the summer of 1935 I became a close "friend" of this buck. I went into his enclosure several times to make close-up pictures. My main difficulty was to keep the deer far enough from me to permit picture making. He seemed to prefer standing by my side, licking my bare arms or rubbing his stubby antlers on my bootlegs. This continued until the 1935 set of antlers were full grown but still "in the velvet." Within the period of a few months I shot several rolls of film—from fifty to seventy-five pictures in all—but only one was what I would call really good. This shot was published in the August 1936 issue of *National Geographic,* with a Great Smokies story written by Leonard C. Roy.

In the meantime, the buck had eaten all of the grass and shrubs back many feet from the fence. Knowing that a picture made on such bare ground would not look very nice; I took some green stuff in with me the next time I tried to get some more pictures. I carried the food back to the edge of the wooded section so I would have green trees as a background. But, before I could get the desired ten feet away, he had eaten the weeds and was back at my side. After several unsuccessful attempts to take in enough weeds to keep him occupied for a minute or two, I saw a man from the hotel kitchen coming up with a paper bag full of bread scraps, of which the deer was quite fond.

A deer feeding on scraps

This, I figured, would be my chance to get the desired pictures, at the preferred spot. So, I took the sack of bread scraps with the intention of scattering them on the ground near the edge of the trees. The mistake that I made was that I did not have the cooperation of the hungry buck. It was rather obvious that he thought I was about to run off with his bread, and he made it very clear that he didn't like any part of my plan.

In less time than it takes to tell about it, the buck—my friend, you know—reared to his hind feet and was slashing away at me with his nimble front feet. The sack of bread was scattered in all directions. My camera, with tripod attached, was hanging loosely over my left arm but it, too, was knocked to the ground and badly bent. My left arm was bruised, and he cut two or three slashes into my trousers leg.

Needless to say, I beat a hasty retreat, grabbing my camera while on the run. I climbed that high fence in "nothing flat," and that is the last time that I ever entered the enclosure. The result is that I never got any more pictures of my "old friend," but I am thankful that I had already gotten the exceptionally good one. This all occurred some years before we began to see deer in and near Cades Cove.

In January of 1936, while I was still on good terms with the buck, I found one of his 1935 antlers. He carried the other one for a few weeks, after which, Jim Huff, one of Andy's sons, found it. Jim and I then began trying to get the antler that the other had, and we were both holding out in the hope of getting the full set. I offered to buy Jim's antler, but found him not the least bit interested in selling, and our "bargaining" came to a standstill. In a final desperate effort to gain possession of the 1935 set, I reminded Jim that he was there in Gatlinburg with a good chance to get the 1936 set—but that my only chance for a full set was to get the one he then owned. I reminded him, too, that it would be especially nice for me to own the 1935 set—the same antlers that the buck was wearing when I made the picture that was published in the *Geographic.* That way I could show friends the actual antlers, then the published picture, and let them see that they were the very same antlers. This line of reasoning worked, and Jim gave me his antler, even refusing to let me pay for it.

I never did learn whether or not Jim got the 1936 set of antlers, but I hope so.

Several years later R. T. (Bob) Maher, veteran hiker and fisherman, was sitting on Gregory Bald, about one hundred feet from the edge of the woods. He and a hiking companion were just resting and enjoying the beauty of Gregory Bald. Bob's camera was in his pack, several feet from where they were sitting.

To the very great surprise of both men, a big buck walked out of the woods, came several feet toward where they were sitting, then just stood there looking curiously at the hikers. Bob knew that any move to get his camera would serve only to frighten the deer away, so he just sat there, mentally kicking himself for not having his camera available for such a rare shot. After a few minutes, minutes that seemed much longer than they were, the deer walked on back into the woods—with Bob still bemoaning the fact that his camera was out of reach. It was then too late, he knew. But not so. In less than five minutes the buck walked out onto the bald again, this time coming even closer to the bewildered hikers—whose camera was still out of reach. It's a safe bet that Bob now keeps his camera with him, although it is not likely that he will ever again have such an opportunity to use it.

A few more years later, however, deer were being seen frequently in Cades Cove, just a few at first, then in considerable numbers, but almost always during the late autumn, winter, or early spring months. Early morning was when most of them were seen, with late afternoons as the next best time.

One day, during the first hour of morning light, Mrs. Campbell, Mr. and Mrs. Virgil Tarwater and I saw fifty-six deer. Somewhat smaller numbers were seen on other morning trips over the eleven-mile one-way loop road around the cove. During the last hour of daylight in the afternoons we have on several occasions seen as many as twenty-five in the one-hour trip. During the cool weather seasons we seldom miss seeing at least a few. We have seen herds of twenty-five, eighteen, and ten, but at most times they are seen in smaller numbers.

It is fascinating just to see the deer in the edge of the forests or in the open pasturelands of Cades Cove. Even more interesting is to watch the ease with which they jump fences from five to six feet high. Usually the jumping is done in a graceful, gliding movement at the end of a short run. At times we have seen a buck jump over the fence, with the two or three does that were with him in the edge of the road ducking under the fence. The amazing thing, however, is to see a big buck stand motionless within four or five feet of a fence then spring up and over the fence as though having been shot upward by some unseen external force. They are, indeed, fantastic jumpers.

The Cades Cove deer have not yet completely lost their fear of man, and it is unusual for a person to get any closer than seventy-five to one hundred feet. In the course of time they are likely to appear to be more and more "tame." But, please remember, they are truly wild animals (as I learned), and be governed accordingly.

Bitten by a Rattler

Most people seem to be afraid of snakes—just any snake.

Although a rattlesnake bit me—due entirely to my carelessness, incidentally—I am not afraid of even the poisonous species. It is my conviction that a snake will not strike at a person unless it believes it is being attacked, such as when a person steps too closely to the snake while stepping over a log. Even since I was bitten, I have passed within a few feet of a rattler, and watched it crawl into a hole beside the trail.

While doing more than four thousand miles of Great Smokies hiking, much of it where there was no trail, I can recall seeing only five live rattlers and two or three that had been killed by hikers ahead of me, and only three copperheads. This does not mean that snakes are scarce in the Smokies. There are many of them, I suspect, but there is little chance that a hiker will see one, especially while hiking along a graded trail.

In May of 1935 I made an overnight hike to Greenbrier Pinnacle with a small group of friends, including Mr. and Mrs. West Barber, their daughter Florence, their son Dean, and Miss Evelyn Welch. Through the kindness of the late Mel Price, then on fire lookout duty at the tower, we slept in the ranger's cabin while Mel spent the night on the tower. After a hearty breakfast, we set out for a hike that was to take us a mile or so up the Pinnacle Lead, along which there was no trail.

As Mel stopped with me while I made a picture of Mt. LeConte, the others proceeded on up the ridge. Pretty soon I heard Dean Barber calling to me. "Come and see what we have," he said. But he couldn't wait to tell me what they really had. "We've got a rattlesnake," he added. When Mel and I reached the others, we saw the rattler which they were holding under the end of a forked stick.

Foolishly, I suggested that we tie it up and take it to the Zoology Department at the University of Tennessee. There was no objection, at least at that point. So I removed the string from the lace-leg trousers I was wearing and made a loop in one end. Momentarily being duly cautious, I placed my boot on the snake's neck, just back of the forked stick, as the loop was slipped over the rattler's head and drawn tight, with the other end of the string tied to the stick.

For the purpose of making some pictures, the snake was moved onto a large sloping rock and the pictures snapped. With the snake's head then fifteen or more inches from the end of the stick, it dawned on me that it would be difficult to carry it back down to the ranger's cabin, through the fairly dense underbrush. In retrospect I can think of two *safe* ways in which the head could have been held close to the end of the stick. First, and perhaps easiest, I could have rolled the stick until all of the slack in the string was wrapped around it. Or we could have tied another string around the end of the stick and then pulled up the slack until the "business end" of the reptile was held firmly. Better yet, we could have just left the snake where it was caught—either dead or alive. Those ideas, however, did not come to mind until it was too late to use them.

The solution that I sought to use—over several protests, especially from Miss Welch—was to again place the fork of the stick over the snake's neck, leaving one end of the string around the neck and the other around the end of the stick, thus leaving a loop in the string. Still with protests from Evelyn, I placed my left hand around the string, just back of the forked stick and took the loop in my right hand, endeavoring to tie a knot that would hold the reptile's head close to the stick.

The rattlesnake that bit me on May 5, 1935, as I was trying to take up the slack in the string. This is on the second knob of Pinnacle Lead—a mile above the fire tower on Greenbrier Pinnacle.

Mt. Chapman, Mt. Sequoyah, and Eagle Rocks as seen from porch of cabin on Greenbrier Pinnacle (made on May 5, 1935, after the rattlesnake bite). Spring comes late at this elevation.

Before I could tie the knot, and actually not seeing just what had happened, I felt a sting on the index finger of my right hand. It was quickly evident that I had been bitten. Although my eyes were within twenty-four inches of the snake's head, and although other members of the party were only a few feet away, nobody knows just how it happened. Obviously, the stick, then resting on the big boulder rather than on soft ground, must not have been down tightly against the snake's head. Did it slip out at one end or the other? Or did it merely extend its head a few more inches? We do not know.

Nobody in the group had a snakebite kit, but I realized that I must get out as much of the poison as possible. The pocketknife that I was carrying was not very sharp, as I remembered, so I borrowed West Barber's sharp knife and immediately cut my finger at the location of the bite. I then sucked out the blood and spat it out. This was done several times, after which my bandana was used for a tourniquet.

Mel and I then started down the ridge, approximately a mile to the tower, so he could send a radio message to Gatlinburg for help. The tourniquet was loosened frequently, and each time that was done I sucked and spat out some more of the poison. On the way down Mel told me that he believed he still had a small quantity of whiskey at the cabin. When I told him that a drink of whiskey would only make things worse, he quickly told me it was to be used as an antiseptic. So upon reaching the cabin, he emptied the whiskey into a teacup, and I dipped the three middle fingers of my right hand into the cup of whiskey, holding the cup with the thumb and little finger. In a matter of just a few minutes the poison from the snakebite had turned the whiskey to a definite green color.

🖋 🖋 🖋

Mel sent a radio message to park headquarters telling what had happened. The news was relayed by telephone to the Civilian Conservation Corps Camp in Greenbrier, and within a very few minutes the camp physician, Dr. Miles S. Crowder, and about ten Civilian Conservation Corps enrollees were on the way up to carry me out. In the meantime, I felt no severe pain—just about like from a bee sting—and I climbed part of the way up the fire tower and made some pictures while we waited.

Dr. Stanley A. Cain, then a professor of botany at the University of Tennessee (and later assistant secretary of the Interior under Secretary Stewart L. Udall) was at the CCC camp when the call for help was received. Dr. Cain, a personal friend, was the only man present who knew the snakebite victim, so he joined the "rescue" party. The CCC boys, naturally annoyed by the emergency created by my carelessness, weren't trying to set any speed records as they climbed the Pinnacle Trail. Dr. Cain, much more interested, was not satisfied with the slow pace they had set, and he soon took the stretchers and set out ahead of the others. In fact, he negotiated the four miles of fairly steep trail in about one hour—which meant that he must have run part of the way.

When he arrived at the tower, he and Mel Price conferred for a moment, after which I was told to get on the stretcher. I protested, with the remark that I felt as well as either of them, and perhaps better than Stanley, who must have been tired. The next I heard was Mel's very firm and serious voice as he said, "Are you going to get on, or do you want me to put you on?" There was no mistaking the fact that he meant exactly what he said, so I got on the stretcher, and Stanley and Mel started down the trail with me.

We had gone almost a mile before we met any of the CCC boys, after which they took over the carrying job. As we met other boys, they relieved those who had been doing the carrying, and for the rest of the trip they alternated regularly. It was almost another mile before we met Dr. Crowder. He made a hurried examination, which included questions as to the possibility of any nausea, increased heart action, etc. He then did some more cutting on my finger, making an "X" mark, whereas I had made only one straight cut. He also sought to get some suction by using a metal suction cup, which he pressed firmly against my finger. Of course, the shape of my finger made it impossible to get suction. And, incidentally, the most severe pain that I experienced was when he bore down on that suction cup. By that time there was considerable swelling, especially on the back of my hand and in my forearm. Dr. Crowder watched the swelling carefully, and soon announced that if it got worse, he might have to cut my hand to relieve the swelling.

At this point I must digress a bit and report that just three days earlier I had carried our fine bull dog to the car so he could be taken to the veterinarian to see what was wrong with him. When the vet saw that the dog had a case of "dumb" rabies, he sent me, and other members of the family who had handled the dog, to take rabies shots. This was a safety measure because some rabies germs might have gotten into possible scratches or other breaks in our skin. I was, therefore, scheduled to take another rabies shot that same afternoon when I returned from the Greenbrier Pinnacle hike.

Now, back to Dr. Crowder and his examination. He did not then know of my prescribed rabies treatment. He had explained that any cutting done to relieve the swelling might leave me with a stiff hand. When he decided that another incision was not indicated, he said that we would go on down to the camp and eat lunch, after which he would send me to Knoxville in a CCC pickup truck, and that I could go to my own doctor for any needed further treatment.

"That sounds like a good idea," I told him, "because I have to go to my doctor this afternoon to get another rabies shot."

The air was a bit blue, with language that Dr. Crowder didn't learn at Sunday school. "Bitten by a mad dog, then bitten by a rattlesnake," he exclaimed. "The best thing I can think of is to knock you in the head and throw you over the cliff." His attitude was only slightly softened when he was told that the dog had not bitten me—and that the rabies shots were only precautionary.

By the time I reached home, and my doctor's office, my hand and forearm were about twice normal size. Luckily, my family doctor agreed with Dr. Crowder that it would not be necessary to do any more cutting. There was very little pain remaining, but I did lose the fingernail and most of the skin from that index finger.

Several things doubtless had a bearing on the fact that the effects were not too serious. In the first place, the back of one's finger is perhaps the least dangerous of all places for a bite, there being so little circulation at that point. Another helpful fact is that the snake had struck at nearby sticks several times before it bit me, and thus dissipated much of its supply of poison.

At that time I was spending a good part of my time writing stores about the Great Smokies for newspapers and magazines. Since my typing had always been by the hunt and peck system, I had always used the two index fingers in my typing. But, following this mishap I had to use the middle finger on my right hand while the index finger was still too sore for such use. Thus, the manuscripts for *Birth of a National Park, Great Smoky Mountains Wildflowers,* and all later writing was done with the index finger of my left hand and the middle finger of the right hand.

A few weeks after my snake bite—which was really not the snake's fault—Mr. Price sent the rattles to me "as a souvenir." A friend, hearing that the snake had been killed, remarked that it seemed to be a waste of effort. "It would have died anyway," he added. He was referring to the fact that men who were building trails and making the preliminary grades for park roads found and killed large numbers of snakes, especially rattlers. Although it is possible that a few of them might have been bitten, I do not recall having heard of any such mishaps.

The only other man I personally know to have been bitten in the Great Smokies was the late W. P. "Buck" Toms. Many years ago, possibly as far back as the prepark days, Buck was climbing up the almost sheer wall of rock at the left of Abrams Falls. He made the mistake of reaching up and placing one hand within a few inches of a rattler—which, of course, bit him. He suffered no serious consequences from the bite.

✍   ✍   ✍

One of the first of several park regulations announced was that of "no hunting." While on a hike in the Greenbrier wilderness area, I found a few empty shotgun shells on and near the trail. Feeling that hunters had been busy in that seldom visited part of the park, I turned them in at the park office as evidence.

My attention was called to the fact that the shells were for a small-bore gun, and that it had been used by a research scientist rather than by hunters. They did, however, instruct the scientist to bring back all of his empty shells in the future so that they might not cause others actually to do some hunting there.

The scientist was Dr. E. V. Komarek, who was working under the sponsorship of the Chicago Academy of Science, with full approval of the National Park Service, in return for information and specimens that he was to turn over to the park. Dr. Komarek, often with assistance from his brother, Roy V. Komarek, was seeking to find and identify as many species of birds and animals as possible. To do this accurately, he had to collect a few of each species so they could be positively identified. Various species of snakes were also collected by Dr. Komarek, but usually not by shooting them.

On May 5, 1929, Dr. Komarek was the speaker for a meeting of the hiking club, as a part of the club's educational program. During the course of his talk, when he referred to snakes, a member of the audience expressed surprise when he learned that Dr. Komarek did not kill every rattlesnake he saw. This remark brought forth a statement from Dr. Komarek that was quite a surprise to most of the assembled hikers. After the general statement that the animal life of a region is like a web, he told us, "if you destroy one strand of the web you disturb the balance of all the others."

"For instance, the rattlesnake feeds largely on certain small mice," he said. "If rattlesnakes were all killed, or drastically reduced in number, these mice would multiply until they became pests. These mice live largely on the taproots of young trees. If the rattlers should be exterminated, or even thinned out too much, the mice would become so numerous that the forests would soon be killed off, and reforestation would be futile," he continued. "It has been shown over and over again that when any species is disturbed or eliminated from a region, some other species expands to take its place."

He admitted that, although rattlesnakes are dangerous, any hiker is likely to see very few of them, and that by being alert the danger is very slight. He then stressed the point that the rattler does much more good than harm, and that it was his general rule to not kill them.

"There was one exception, however," he added. "Once I was crawling through a clump of rhododendron on hands and knees. As I looked up, I saw a rattler staring me in the eye from an uncomfortably short distance.

Then I repealed my general rule as I blew the snake's head off with my gun. It was the only thing to do, as I was in a very compromising position."

Even so, most visitors to the Smokies are deathly afraid of snakes, and especially the rattlers and copperheads. It would be a bit difficult for them to realize that we could not have our fine forests—one of the main assets of the Smokies—except for the constant work of the rattlers in keeping the mice under control.

Boomers

Most animals learn rather quickly when man ceases to be an archenemy and, instead, becomes friend.

An interesting illustration of this fact was witnessed and enjoyed by a group of hikers of which I was a member during a lunch period at Alum Cave Bluff about 1935. Bits of unwanted food, especially bread scraps, were tossed away. In a matter of a very few minutes, several boomers—small red squirrels—were eating these food scraps. As we watched the boomers, we began throwing the food closer and closer, until they were feeding within ten or twelve feet of us.

At that stage of the game, there was no rivalry between the boomers—each one ate what he found, without any disturbance from the others. All of a sudden the scene changed drastically. One of the most daring, which had come somewhat closer to us than the others, discovered a large supply of cookies in the open end of my hiking pack. After his lucky find he immediately "staked a claim" on the contents of my pack. Any other squirrel that dared come close was immediately chased away.

After nibbling on a cookie for a moment, he evidently realized that he could not eat all of my supply there and then. He again drove off all potential poachers from his territory, then carried a cookie away into the underbrush and apparently hid it. He came back quickly, checked the immediate surroundings for possible intruders, and carried another tidbit to his secret storehouse.

Each time he carried off a cookie, some of us moved a foot or two closer to my pack. These short moves did not disturb the cookie thief, and very soon I was within five feet of my pack without causing any interruption to his activities. In the meantime, the other bushy tails contented themselves with the scattered food scraps that some of the generous hikers kept providing. But the one that had discovered and commandeered my intended dessert kept up his removals until the last cookie was gone.

In the foregoing epistle the boomers provided both the plot and the acting. A few weeks later, however, Jim Thompson and I decided to see if we could stage a repeat performance at the end of Clingmans Dome Road, which is about twenty miles from the previous "stage." We had often seen the diminutive squirrels feeding on the steep slopes just below the road level.

On our return from a hike to Silers Bald we found the boomers at the end of the road, as expected, but they were being harassed by some men who were tossing pebbles, rather than food, and we feared that our plans were ruined. We quickly stopped the pebble tossing, although one of the men seemed to think it was none of our business.

In this experiment we had a double objective. We wanted, of course, to see if the boomer that found the big supply of cookies would drive off any other that dared to intrude. Also, we wanted to get a close-up picture of the bushy tail as he started to carry off a cookie.

Finding two small boulders that were about the right distance apart and some fifteen feet below the edge of the parking area, I placed my hiking pack on one boulder, with the big supply of cookies in plain sight. I marked off a spot on the other boulder that was a measured four feet away, which was to be the location of my camera. I then returned to the edge of the parking area and started scattering pieces of cookies on the bank below me, thus luring the boomers closer and closer to my pack. Here, again, there was no evidence of fighting or other friction.

When the lucky boomer made his discovery, the same pattern of behavior that we had witnessed at Alum Cave Bluff was repeated before our eyes. He immediately chased off any "poacher" that came too close. He, too, carried the cookie off and hid it, then returned for another. While he was off on that brief trip, I moved a foot or two nearer to where I was to sit while attempting to make the picture.

After about a dozen such moves I was sitting on the selected boulder with the camera held firmly on the marked spot. Although the distance of my latest move was no more than those before it, there was another difference that seemed to disturb the "actor." On the earlier moves I remained standing. On this last move I was seated. He hesitated a moment, then approached the cookies from the opposite side of the pack—whereas on his earlier trips he had walked over the pack to the cookie supply. I was afraid that this difference might ruin the chance for a good picture, but not so. After taking the cookie in his mouth, he walked up over the pack, as in previous trips, but actually paused for a brief moment, as if to say, "All right, go ahead and snap your picture," which I did.

The whole experiment consumed only about fifteen minutes. As I was luring the boomers toward my pack, and during the maneuvering that followed, Jim was making movies of the whole scene. Before it was over, we

A "boomer" (small red squirrel) steals cookies from my backpack.

had quite an interested gallery, which included the men who, a few minutes earlier, had been throwing rocks at the friendly little boomers.

Park maintenance crews were removing a tree that had been blown across the Newfound Gap Highway during a heavy windstorm. In sawing the tree into short lengths so they could be carried off more easily, a nest of young boomers was found in a hollow section of the tree. John Morrell, then a supervisory ranger but later a special assistant to the superintendent, found a baby, possibly about two weeks old, with eyes not yet opened. He felt that it did not have much chance for survival if left there, so he took it home with him and started feeding it from a medicine dropper. John's formula was so successful that the squirrel thrived on it and soon was able to start eating peanuts. Being a red squirrel, and "rufus" being Latin for red, the baby was given the name of Rufus. John trained the pet to come to him when he called, "Come, Rufus; come, Rufus," and his reward for answering that call was a feast of peanuts.

During the sixty-three days that John kept Rufus at his home a great friendship developed. As John returned from work each day he made sure that he had plenty of peanuts in his pockets, and Rufus was soon eating from his hands.

Although this was an enjoyable arrangement, both for members of the Morrell family and for Rufus, John knew that the relationship must be terminated and Rufus returned to his native habitat. Accordingly, John took the pet boomer back to the same location where it had been found. There, he again fed peanuts to Rufus and gave him his freedom.

It was thirteen days after the release before Rufus answered John's calls. Later visits ranged from three to sixteen days apart. John reported contacts having been made on thirty-one different days, out of a total of forty attempted meetings.

"On Sunday, December 2, 1956 I spent 40 minutes with Rufus," John told me. "He took peanuts from my hand and buried them in the snow."

Romance had entered the picture a bit earlier. "Rufus introduced his mate a few days later. Both little boomers ate from my hand, but Rufus didn't seem to like the idea and tried to drive the mate away," John related. On the several following visits, both answered my calls, and Rufus always ate from my hand, but he wouldn't let her come that close anymore."

The last time John saw either Rufus or "Mrs. Rufus" was on January 6, 1957, although several later attempts were made. John always left peanuts on a feeding board that had been used, but they were not disturbed. It is John's guess that a hawk probably caught him.

Thus ends a true story that proved a delight for my young grandchildren for many months. For some years later, when the grandchildren saw a log or tree in which there was an opening, they would say, "That is where Rufus's cousin lives." So, although Rufus is long gone, he still has "cousins" that provide enjoyment for the children.

Although other animals are perhaps more numerous than the deer and bears, many of them are nocturnal and very shy, with the result that park visitors seldom get to see even one of them. In forty-three years of rather intensive visits to all parts of the Smokies, I have seen only two bobcats, two foxes, one mink, and three raccoons.

Two of the raccoons came to the Moores Spring trail shelter, near Gregory Bald, just after dark one night. Before seeing them, we could hear them as they moved cautiously through the underbrush near the shelter. We threw pieces of bread toward where they were, and soon they were lured to the edge of the shrubs, thus giving us a dim view of them. The bread scraps were then thrown somewhat nearer to where we were sitting, as quietly as we could. Since we were not moving, they came to within about ten feet of us, which enabled Jim Thompson to get a good flash picture of them. A bit frightened by the brilliance of the flash, it was several minutes before they came—from a different direction—within camera range, which permitted making another good flash shot of them.

Insofar as we knew, or thought, they then went away. If so, it was only a temporary departure, but it was not until we were preparing breakfast the next morning that we learned for certain that they had come back some time during the night, and that they had carried off every bit of our bread.

Other animals believed to have inhabited the Smokies or surrounding foothills, but which the park naturalists believe have not been seen for at least one hundred years, include elk, beaver, and wolf. A few reports of wolves have been circulated, and by many people believed, but the naturalists still express serious doubt.

SIGHTS TO SEE

Destinations of many popular hikes are some of the numerous waterfalls and cascades of the Great Smokies, especially those on the Tennessee side of the park. Four of the most heavily visited and most beautiful of these scenic displays of water are Rainbow Falls, on the north slope of Mt. LeConte; Laurel Falls, on the trail between Fightin' Creek Gap and Cove Mountain; Abrams Falls, most easily reached from the west end of Cades Cove; and Ramsey Cascades, in the Greenbrier wilderness area.

Rainbow Falls, approximately four miles from Cherokee Orchard and halfway to the top of LeConte, is normally just a slender ribbon of water making a plunge of about seventy feet. But after a hard rain or a prolonged general rain, it becomes a spectacular display of turbulent water. Its most unique appearance, however, is in the winter when the temperature has been below freezing for several consecutive days. On January 28, 1940, Guy Frizzell, Dutch Roth, and I left Knoxville in zero weather for a special hike to Rainbow Falls. In Gatlinburg, Chief Park Naturalist Arthur Stupka joined us. The thermometer had been well below freezing for a week or more, and we expected and hoped to find two huge ice cones at the falls— one built up from the bottom and the other an inverted cone hanging from the top. We even hoped that the two cones might have met, or nearly so, thus forming an icy "hour glass."

When we parked the car at Cherokee Orchard, we found a few inches of snow covering the ground. We had dressed warmly because of the severe cold at Knoxville. As soon as we entered the forest, we were trudging through six inches of snow, except for Stupka, who was wearing snowshoes. There wasn't a cloud in the sky, and no wind. With the reflected heat from the snow, we began to peel off the extra coats and sweaters and were quite comfortable hiking along in our shirtsleeves.

Upon reaching our destination we found that the lower cone had built up to a height of about thirty or thirty-five feet. The top one, however, was much shorter. We could see that the suspended icicles were more slender and not so long. Remnants of other upper cones were seen around the base of the lower. The direct and reflected heat at the top of the upper cones had caused them to break loose and fall; otherwise the two certainly would have met. Even though there was some ten feet between them, it was a thrilling and unusual sight.

Both of the cones were hollow, with the main body of the stream still flowing through the center. The icicles were formed around the main stream as splashing water froze to the rocks. After a day or so there was a ring of ice all around the stream of water. Then, as small portions of the stream continued to hit the edge of the ice ring, the icicle grew into a huge hollow ice cone.

A hike to Rainbow Falls is strongly recommended after a week or more of below-freezing weather.

Without any doubt the waterfall that is most frequently visited by hikers is Laurel Falls, which is 1.3 miles from the parking area at Fightin' Creek Gap, on Highway 73. Part of the popularity of this hike is the short distance, but there are other reasons. It is really two falls, one of which drops down to the edge of the Cove Mountain trail, while the other plunges off below the trail. Pictures usually show only the upper fall because it can be made as a close-up, whereas the photographer has to get so far away in order to get both falls in the picture, that it is much less interesting. Another reason so many visitors like this hike is because of the fine views that are provided along the way, especially the views of Blanket Mountain and Miry Ridge.

Many women, having heard about the beauty and interest of Laurel Falls, and realizing it is a relatively short walk, made the trip wearing high-heel shoes. This unwise practice led the Park Service to blacktop this trail. Even with the smooth surface it is not safe to hike that far—2.6 miles round-trip—in high heels. It is likely that many women have made that discovery the hard way.

Abrams Falls, two and a half miles from Cades Cove, is not as high as the other popular falls, but the much larger volume of water makes up for the lack of height. This large stream has carved out a very deep pool and has thus created an exceptionally good "swimming hole," one of the very best in the entire park. It is, in fact, so deep that very few swimmers are able to touch bottom even when diving from the top of the falls. Herman Silva Forest—known best to hiking companions as "Foozy," is the only person I have seen reach the bottom of the pool, and he had made several unsuccessful dives before he was able to do it.

The level "benches" of solid rock near the base of the waterfall are favorite picnic sites and are also good places for swimmers and divers to sun themselves while resting.

Rainbow Falls—plunging eighty-three feet over the rugged cliff beside the "Rainbow Falls–Rocky Spur Trail" to Mt. LeConte. Note the hikers behind the lacy falls, July 7, 1934. This is the normal size of the falls, but it becomes a raging torrent after heavy rains.

A mid-winter view of Rainbow Falls after three weeks of continuous cold weather, January 28, 1940. The bottom "cone" reaches a height of about thirty to thirty-five feet.

Laurel Falls, the most frequently visited waterfall, on May 26, 1935. It is 1.3 miles from the parking area at Fightin' Creek Gap on Highway 73.

This is the upper portion of Ramsey Cascades, April 15, 1938. It is the most beautiful and picturesque natural display of water it has been my good fortune to see.

This rocky cliff was a sheer sheet of solid ice, with the stream falling behind the ice. Note the leaves of the rhododendron on the left, sometimes called "nature's thermometer" because the leaves droop and close up during extremely cold weather.

The "Sinks"—beautiful falls and a deep pool under the bridge on Scenic Loop Highway (near the Blount–Sevier county line) on July 4, 1934. The new Park Service trail to Meigs Mountain starts here.

Large quantities of trailing arbutus (*Epigea repens*) may be seen along this trail in March and early April. I do not know any other spot or trailside in the whole park that offers so much of this delicately beautiful and early-blooming wildflower. This trail is also lined with fine stands of mountain laurel (*Kalmia latifolia*). The peak blooming season, a bit earlier here than in higher elevations, is in May and June, with occasional flowers as early as April.

Although Ramsey Cascades has not been as heavily visited as the others have, it is my pick of the well-known waterfalls and cascades of the entire park insofar as sheer beauty and charm is concerned. As the name implies, it is not an actual waterfall, but an extremely steep series of dashing, splashing cascades. I have seen two-thousand-foot ribbons of water in the Canadian Rockies, but to me Ramsey Cascades is the most beautiful and picturesque natural display of water it has been my good fortune to see. In fact, I know of no other spot in the Smokies that is quite as beautiful as the one I behold as I stand on or near the foot log just below the cascades. It is beautiful throughout the year. I have seen it when that rocky cliff was a sheer sheet of solid ice, with the stream falling behind the ice.

There is an element of considerable danger, however, for hikers who get too close to the brow of any waterfall, and doubly so at the top of Ramsey Cascades. The solid rock over which the water flows just before starting the downward plunge slopes gently toward the edge of the cliff. Although splashing water keeps the rocks from moist to wet much of the time, the beauty of the view from the top of Ramsey Cascades lures many visitors dangerously close to the edge.

On July 28, 1962, Louise Barber, the fifteen-year-old daughter of Mr. and Mrs. David W. Barber and granddaughter of Mr. and Mrs. D. West Barber, lost her life in a fall from the top of these cascades. Several years earlier a young man, James E. Wolfkiel, Jr., also fell from the same ledge, but was more fortunate; he didn't even have any broken bones.

Hikers visiting any of the Great Smokies waterfalls should remember that the top of any waterfall or steep cascade is an extremely dangerous place. Also, they should know that the view from several feet back is almost as good—maybe just as good—as from the dangerous edge.

Still another waterfall—or, rather, a very steep cascade—is on Mill Creek about two or three miles south of the southwest corner of Cades Cove. Although it is much taller than the four famous falls and cascades, it remains virtually unknown to most hikers. There is no trail, not even a beaten path, to this distinctive cascade. Dr. Randolph Shields, head of the Biology Department of Maryville College and a native of Cades Cove, serves as a seasonal naturalist during the summer months. On infrequent occasions he takes a few hardy hikers to see Mill Creek Cascade, but he usually makes the approach by a different route each time so as not to make a beaten path.

Many park visitors can never see Rainbow Falls, Abrams Falls, or Ramsey Cascades, and even Laurel Falls is too difficult for a few of them. Fortunately, however, there are some treats available for them—water displays they may enjoy from their automobile. Motorists driving up through Little River Gorge (Tennessee Highway 73 from Townsend toward Elkmont and Gatlinburg) have the privilege of seeing one beautiful waterfall and a low but interesting cascade. Meigs Falls, on Meigs Creek just before that stream empties into Little River, can be seen without getting out of the car. Parking space for several cars has been provided for the use of those who want to linger or to make pictures.

The cascade, designated as the Sinks, is a mile farther up Little River. As at Abrams Falls, the large volume of water has carved out a deep pool. The swirling water makes it quite hazardous, and at least one death has occurred there. Even so, the pool is a popular swimming and diving spot. The turbulent water at the Sinks and in the stream above the cascade can not be seen very well from an automobile, but parking spaces for several cars have been provided. It is recommended that for the best views, every visitor to this beauty spot should go to the bridge, and to the opposite bluffs just below the cascade.

✺   ✺   ✺

Since the volume of Little River varies greatly throughout the year, Mrs. Campbell and I often select a time when there has been more or less constant rain for two or three days for a trip to the Sinks. On such a day, when it was still raining, I told office associates that we were heading for the Sinks.

"In all this rain?" one of the men asked.

"Because of the rain," I replied.

It was a most rewarding trip. Seldom had we seen so much turbulence in the swollen stream. In places the water came to within a few inches of the road level, and we learned later that a short section of the road was flooded shortly after we were there. It was a majestic sight that we saw at the Sinks. We had on many previous visits seen that cascade with everything from a very small stream on up to a raging torrent—but never before quite so much water. The view from the bluffs was as thrilling as we had expected. The real treat this time was to stand on the bank, or the bridge, and watch the "back side" of water hitting a ledge about halfway down the cascade. It then bounded up some six or eight feet before it completed a big arch and fell back into the stream at the bottom of the cascade. The front, or downstream, side was a mass of madly whirling and splashing water. That was the most spectacular phase. But, to us, far more interesting was the glassy smoothness of the back, or upstream, side, of the arching water. As we looked into it, we could see that the water was heavily charged with small rocks—from the size of a man's fist on down. We could see that it was but a few inches from one of these rocks to another. Then, realizing that the entire stream was heavily loaded with such rocks, and seeing the swiftness of the stream, we could easily see how those riverbeds had been carved or dug out through the countless years that such high water had been at work. As a small boy I had often wondered how the rounded stones that we knew as river rocks had been formed. Watching such sights as we witnessed that day it was easy to see how the rough edges of broken bits of boulders would be torn off when carried for considerable distances each time there was such high water.

A friend, having heard about our experience on that day, remarked to his wife that he had often wondered why they never saw the interesting things that the Campbells so often saw. Then it dawned upon him that it may be because the Campbells go to the mountains more often, and that perhaps they had learned the best times to witness such interesting sights.

What, in your opinion, is the most beautiful spot in the Great Smoky Mountains National Park?

Admittedly, most answers to that question would list one or more of the vantage points that provide breathtaking panoramas. Or, perhaps, you might be inclined to prefer a location where one can see acres of purple rhododendron during the peak blooming season; or a place from which the extravaganza of autumn colors may be seen most advantageously.

That, however, is not the type of beauty spots that I have in mind in connection with the question. The reference is to any small area, possibly not more than one hundred yards in diameter, where the sheer charm and beauty is the dominant feature. It is at such locations that many visitors might like to linger, in quiet meditation, for an hour or so because of the soul-satisfying experience thus provided.

Through the years I have asked many fellow hikers to tell me their favorite beauty spots of this nature. And, of course, I have made mental notes of my own preferences. With the hope that it might help others to discover the picturesque qualities of such locations, a few of them are listed herewith—not necessarily in the order of preference.

Many visitors are advised to see "the big tree" on the trail between Cades Cove and Gregory Bald. To me, however, the visitor who hikes *only* the mile and a half to that one six-foot tulip poplar gets cheated. The next half mile is much more rewarding, in my opinion, and the best of all is what can be seen while standing on the second footbridge above the big tree and looking back down the trail. There is no single tree as large as "the big tree," but there are several almost as large—rising from a beautiful undercover of rhododendron. To me, there are few—if any—spots in the whole park with more real natural beauty.

A close second in my list of favorites is the spectacular display of water at Ramsey Cascades and the immediately surrounding forest. This highly pleasing scene may be enjoyed either from the footbridge just below the cascade, or from the ledge at the right.

Another treat, unfortunately missed by most of those who hike to Ramsey Cascades, is the series of deep pools and smaller cascades that may be seen about a half mile farther upstream. Early hikers knew one of these quiet pools as Drink-water Pool.

A point that is much easier to reach, and which is a favorite for many visitors, is the view looking upstream from the second footbridge on the trail to Chimney Tops, the one that crosses the stream known as Road Prong. Many hikers stop here just to drink in some of the picturesque beauty.

Thousands of hikers each year enjoy the views and sunrises from Myrtle Point of Mt. LeConte. Many of them, however, would find an equally pleasing experience at a quiet little spot about one hundred yards down the ridge to the north. There the ground is still covered by a lush growth of mountain myrtle, just as was Myrtle Point in prepark days. This intimate little spot has a beauty all its own, but it is made even more enjoyable by the dramatic quality of the surroundings.

The Spruce-Fir Nature Trail, reached from Clingmans Dome Road, is distinctive for several reasons—especially the overall beauty of the Canadian-type forest. An added interest is given by the numerous moss-covered logs and small boulders along the way, and the abundance of ferns.

The Cherokee Orchard–Roaring Fork Motor Nature Trail has many attractions. One of these is the fine virgin forest of hemlock trees. Marker Number 5, which corresponds with a paragraph of the descriptive folder, gives the location. The larger trees here are centuries old, and interested motorists should get out and walk through or around these majestic trees.

Marker Number 15, at the last bridge on the Cherokee Orchard–Roaring Fork Motor Nature Trail, justifies parking the car and taking a good look at this interesting spot. Stand on the bridge and look upstream, watching the stream flow across the jagged rocks and into the quiet and deep pool just before flowing under the bridge. Then, stand on the other side of the bridge and watch the swirling water as it dashes wildly over or between huge boulders that line the streambed. Look across the stream at the interesting moss-covered boulders, especially the one where a sizable tree rests on the sharp top of one of the large boulders. To many, the greater interest at this stop comes from looking at the sheer cliff, more than one hundred feet high, which is at the immediate left of the road. Although I make this trip a few times each year, I still find it virtually impossible to pass Station Number 15 without a stop of several minutes.

Some forty years ago I asked Marshall Wilson to tell me his favorite beauty spot of the Smokies. When he told me that it was Porters Flats, I asked why he liked that spot so much. He said that it was because of the number of extra large trees, and the canopy of tree branches overhead. On my first visit I was a bit disappointed. I must have expected to see so many big trees growing so close together that one almost would have to turn sideways to pass between them. But on later visits I learned to appreciate the natural beauty of Porters Flats that Marshall had described.

"The Cherry Orchard," through which one passes en route to Ramsey Cascades, has a similar charm to that of Porters Flats, but has an extra point of interest. Here, the forest is made up largely of huge specimens of black cherry trees, many of them more than three feet in diameter. The first time I heard about "The Cherry Orchard," I supposed it to be an abandoned fruit orchard, and did not recognize it on my first trip to the area. Admittedly, a three-foot tree is not large, even in comparison with the tulip poplars, hemlocks, and other trees of the Smokies. But it is a very large size for black cherry trees. Lumber sawed from black cherry trees—cut from areas outside the park, of course—is used in the manufacture of fine furniture. It is one of the most expensive woods grown in or near the Smokies. The only other species with a comparable value is the black walnut. Hikers en route to Ramsey Cascades will see a few larger trees, especially three very large tulip poplars at the immediate trailside, and a few large buckeyes and hemlocks. But, for sheer beauty of the open forest of "sizable" trees, "The Cherry Orchard" is worthy of special note.

It would be easy, of course, to expand this list of beauty spots to more than twice this number. But the ones I've described here are some of my personal favorites, and I suspect that other visitors to the Great Smokies will find them as enchanting as I have.

BIBLIOGRAPHY

Other phases of interest concerning the Great Smokies are presented in the following selected list of books.

Campbell, Carlos C. *Birth of a National Park in the Great Smoky Mountains.* Knoxville: University of Tennessee Press, 1984.

Campbell, Carlos C., William F. Hutson, Hershal L. Macon, and Aaron J. Sharp. *Great Smoky Mountains Wildflowers.* Fourth edition. Knoxville: University of Tennessee Press, 1988.

Campbell, Carlos C., William F. Hutson, Aaron J. Sharp, and Robert W. Hutson. *Great Smoky Mountains Wildflowers.* Revised and expanded fifth edition. Northbrook, Ill.: Windy Pines Publishing, 1995.

Huheey, James E., and Arthur Stupka. *Amphibians and Reptiles of Great Smoky Mountains National Park.* Knoxville: University of Tennessee Press, 1967.

Stupka, Arthur. *Great Smoky Mountains National Park Natural History Handbook.* Series No. 5. Washington, D.C.: U.S. Government Printing Office, 1960.

———. *Notes on the Birds of Great Smoky Mountains National Park.* Knoxville: University of Tennessee Press, 1963.

———. *Trees, Shrubs, and Woody Vines of Great Smoky Mountains National Park.* Knoxville: University of Tennessee Press, 1964.

———. *Wildflowers in Color.* New York: Harper & Row, 1965.

Thornburgh, Laura. *The Great Smoky Mountains.* Knoxville: University of Tennessee Press, 1967.

Carlos C. Campbell was born August 6, 1892, in the Sevier County community of Kodak, within site of Mt. LeConte.

After his reluctant first hike to Mt. LeConte in October 1924, Mr. Campbell was hooked. His enthusiasm for the mountains that was sparked that day was extinguished only by his death in 1978, at age eighty-six.

Largely through his efforts as manager of the Knoxville Chamber of Commerce in the 1920s, the Smokies became known to the nation. He pressed relentlessly for establishing these rugged mountains as a national park. Mr. Campbell promoted the Smokies so much that he eventually lost his Chamber of Commerce job due to the pressure of some who felt that he should have spent more time bringing industry into the area. One of his last promotions of the park effort before he left the Chamber was the direction of fund-raising to bring the entire Tennessee General Assembly to see the Great Smokies. A result of this effort was the purchase of the first large tract of land for the park.

He was a charter member of the Great Smoky Mountains Conservation Association, which was formed in 1923 to promote the establishment of a national park and now serves to protect and promote its interest. Mr. Campbell served on the board of directors continually from 1930 and served as secretary from 1941 until his death in 1978.

He was also a founding member of the Smoky Mountains Hiking Club. The club was a result of the first hike to Mt. LeConte in 1924. He and other members of this club later established and marked the route of the Appalachian Trail through the park.

In the late 1950s he took several months off work at Provident Mutual Insurance Company to write *Birth of a National Park*. First published in 1960, the book tells the history of the fight to establish the park. It is now in the fourth printing of the fourth edition.

He was coauthor with William F. Hutson and Dr. A. J. Sharp of the very popular book *Great Smoky Mountains Wildflowers,* first published in 1962. The authors elected to receive no royalties from sales of the book in order to keep the purchase price as low as possible so that more people might be able to enjoy it. It was recently rereleased in 1997, after having been expanded and revised for the fifth time.

Mr. Campbell became an avid photographer, making thousands of Great Smokies pictures, and over half of them were published in newspapers and magazines. He was especially proud of his pictures that the prestigious *National Geographic* magazine published. He had a huge collection of color slides of the Great Smokies and would give slide presentations about the park to civic clubs, church groups, and anyone else who asked, never charging a penny for this service.

Carlos C. Campbell's work for the park has certainly not gone unnoticed or unrecognized. The American Scenic Historic Preservation Society presented to him in 1966 its annual Horace Marden Albright Scenic Preservation Medal for his outstanding work in conservation. He was the tenth person to receive the award. Other recipients have been Laurance Rockefeller (son of John D. Rockefeller, Jr.), Ladybird Johnson, wife of the late president Lyndon B. Johnson, and Stuart Udall, former secretary of the interior. In 1973 Mr. Campbell became the twenty-first honorary national park ranger. This award is the highest given by the National Park Service to civilians.

Following his death in 1978, the Great Smoky Mountains Conservation Association established the Carlos C. Campbell Memorial Research Fellowship at the University of Tennessee, honoring his considerable efforts toward establishing the national park. In October 1981, after a suggestion by the Great Smoky Mountains Conservation Association, the National Park Service dedicated the Carlos C. Campbell Overlook in recognition of his long and diligent service. This overlook is located approximately two miles south of Sugarlands Visitor Center, and offers a magnificent view of the valley of the West Prong of Little Pigeon River and the western slopes of Mt. LeConte to Bullhead and Balsam Point.

INDEX

Abercrombie and Fitch, 98

Abrams Falls, xviii, 9, 10, 189, 198, 199, 204

Aconitum uncinatum, 167

Aiken, Ruth, 41

Akron, OH, 15, 91

Albright, Horace Marden, 212

Alexander, Eben, Jr., 151

Alexander, Tom, Jr., x

Alley, Felix, x

Allium tricoccum, 96

Almond, NC, 76

Alum Cave, 156

Alum Cave Bluff, 8, 13, 52, 125, 132, 192, 193

Alum Cave Bluff Parking Area, 12, 151

Alum Cave Bluff Trail, 55, 151, 155

Alum Cave Creek, 63, 155

Alum Cave Parking Area, 12, 65, 100

Alum Cave Trail, 65

American Forests, x, 13, 20, 31

American Rifleman, x, 170, 175

American Scenic Historic Preservation Society, 212

Anderson, Joel H., Jr., 99

Anderson Road, 115, 119

Andre, Frank, 69

Andrews Bald, vii, xviii, 161, 167

Andrews, Forrest, 4

Appalachian Club, 4, 40, 156

Appalachian Trail, v, vii, 22, 26, 28, 29, 47–51, 89, 95, 99, 113, 124, 165, 212

Appalachian Trail Conference, 129

Aralia spinosa, 58

Arch Rock, 65

Argo, Dotty, 41

Asheville, NC, 132

Avery, Bess, 164,

Avery, Myron H., 124

Ayres, John A., 4

Balsam Point, 66, 152, 213

Baltimore, MD, 95

Bankers Trust Company, 39

Barber, Charles I., 4, 5, 8, 9, 163

Barber, David W., 203

Barber, Mrs. David W., 203

Barber, Dean, 184

Barber, Florence, 184

Barber, George F., 5, 9, 76

Barber, Guy L., 9

Barber, Louise, 203

Barber, Mrs. West, 184, 203

Barber, West, 11, 151, 184, 186, 203

Baskins Creek, 106

Battle of King Mountain, 174

Bear Pen Hollow, 13, 66, 100

Behrend, Fred, 41

Bennett, Kelly, xi

Berry, Walter M., 20, 28, 32, 34, 47, 85

Big Creek, 22, 23, 84

Big Meadows, 77

Big Pigeon, 60

Bird, Jesse, 47, 49

Birth of a National Park, ix, xi, 17, 162, 189, 209, 212

Black Camp Gap, 59

Blanket Mountain, 129, 199

Bohn, Frank, 59

Boone, Daniel, 174

Boone, Mary Frank, 41

Bote Mountain, 61, 63, 115, 164

Bote Mountain Trail, 164, 165

Boulevard Ridge, 36, 37

Brackin's cabin, 13

Brewer, Carson, x

Brewster, Rodney L., 42

Bright, Tute, 103

Brightwell, Tom, 104

Brightwell, Walter, 104

Broome, Harvey B., x, 20, 28, 32, 34, 63, 64

Brown, Herrick B., 20, 23, 28, 32, 41

White, Hugh M., 9, 40, 41
Whitney, Shirley Ann, 41
Whittaker, Carter, 20, 25, 28, 32
Whittle Springs Hotel, 39
Wilburn, Donald, 99, 100
Wild East: A Biography of the Great Smoky Mountains, The, ix
Wiles, Harold, 34
Wiley, Joan, 41
Wilson, Frank E., 9, 12, 13
Wilson, Marshall A., 5, 9, 12, 13, 41, 61, 63, 207, 208
Wolfkiel, James E. Jr., 203
Wonderland Park, 5
Wonderment of Mountains, A, x
Woolrich, June, 2
Wooly Tops, 34, 35, 63

Yarnell, Ruby, 42
Yellow Creek Mountain, 51
Yellowstone, 8
YMCA, 5, 64, 76, 90
Yonkers, NY, 157

Zachary, Elsie, 41

Memories of Old Smoky was designed and typeset on a Macintosh computer system using QuarkXPress software. The body text is set in 11/14 Adobe Garamond and display type is set in Mrs. Eaves. This book was typeset by Stephanie Thompson and manufactured by Thomson-Shore, Inc.